Teacher Liability in School-Shop Accidents

Teacher Liability in School-Shop Accidents

Denis J. Kigin, Ed. D.
Professor of Industrial Technology and Dean of University Continuing Education
Arizona State University

PRAKKEN PUBLICATIONS, INC.
Ann Arbor, Michigan

"This publication is designed to provide accurate and authoritative information with regard to the subject matter covered. It is sold with the understanding that the publisher is not engaged in rendering legal, accounting, or other professional advice. If legal advice or other expert assistance is required, the services of a competent professional person should be sought."

—From a Declaration of Principles jointly adopted by a Committe of the American Bar Association and a Committee of Publishers and Associations.

Library of Congress Catalog Card Number 82-061688.

Printed in the United States of America.

ISBN: 0-911168-51-6

TO my wife Helen and to Colleen, Timothy, Kathleen, and Patricia, with gratitude for their understanding and gracious assistance, direct and indirect, in the development and culmination of this work.

Foreword

THIS is an excellent treatise on a subject of increasing public concern. The material will be of assistance to everyone with responsibility in the field of vocational education where the use of machines is required.

Tort liability generally involves claims for damages arising out of personal injury. The rapid development of legal concepts in this area gives importance to a clear analysis of the legal and social problems which arise when accidents occur in school facilities being used for industrial education.

Generally, students involved in accidents of the type covered by this study are minors and, this being the case, it may be anticipated that the problem of school-shop accidents will receive further and more careful attention from legislative bodies, particularly on the local and state levels. This research will form a valuable background for legislative action, and the recommendations for legislative action deserve serious consideration by those responsible for legislation in this field.

I believe that this discussion of the elements of liability, the nature and extent of shop-teacher liability, and the defense of possible litigation, appearing in Chapters 2, 3, and 4, are clearly stated and well documented with the pertinent and controlling authorities. Although not an expert on accident prevention, I think that the recommendations involving the legal ramifications of accident prevention and the section entitled "The Consequences of Liability" are perceptive and reasonable.

I believe that this is an excellent piece of research and commend it to all those interested in this field.

Henry M. Gallagher,
the late Chief Justice,
Minnesota Supreme Court

Introduction

WHILE school shops are potentially dangerous places, they can, when properly equipped, arranged, and managed, provide a relatively safe environment in which youths and adults may work and learn.

In addition to the normal responsibilities of the regular teacher, the shop teacher has the task of maintaining a wide variety of equipment for safe and effective operation. He must provide instruction in the safe use of tools, materials, and equipment. Each school day he must supervise the work of about 100 to 150 energetic and active youths. In short, the problem of the possibility of accidents is one that confronts the shop teacher daily.

Even with the greatest of care, accidents occur occasionally in the school shop. When they do, the teacher or the school, or both, may or may not be liable, depending on a number of conditions prevailing at the time. Naturally, therefore, the shop teacher is interested not only in preventing accidents, but in protecting himself and the school against liability. To this end, he must have facts about legal aspects of shop accidents and the extent and conditions of liability.

This volume, based on extensive research, is almost unique in the literature of the shop teacher. Here are the answers to the whole problem of liability for shop accidents, with recommendations and procedures to follow to safeguard both the teacher and the school.

H. H. London,
Professor Emeritus of Industrial Education,
University of Missouri

Preface

SINCE the first edition of this text appeared in 1963, a number of important changes have occurred within the realm of teacher liability. Some were reflected in the 1973 revision. The current edition continues the task of presenting a comprehensive update. New developments, legislation, and court decisions have all contributed to a variety of intepretations of the law as it relates to litigation growing out of student injuries. The precise impact of the Williams-Steiger Occupational Safety and Health Act of 1970 on school shops and laboratories is yet to be realized.

A basic understanding of school law as it applies to teacher liability becomes increasingly important each year. Teachers have become particularly vulnerable to charges of negligence brought by pupils. A marked responsibility rests with those teachers who instruct in disciplines where students are asked to work with materials, machines, and equipment as a part of the learning process. These teachers not only have the duty to supervise carefully, but have the additional duty of instructing the students in the proper use of equipment. As expected, a high priority should be given to the safety and welfare of the students.

It has been stated that elementary school pupils are in need of continuous supervision; junior-high-aged youngsters, firm direction; high school students, a degree of flexibility; and college and university undergraduates are entitled to increasing independence while engaged in educational pursuits. However, this concept should be treated with caution in light of the specific subject matter taught and the expected level of personal involvement. There are those curriculums that transcend the norm, placing a higher degree of accountability on both students and teachers. Such is the case with respect to vocational, industrial, and technical education.

This is an attempt to provide some assistance for public school industrial education teachers in understanding some of the basic precepts of teacher liability. Its value could be extended to school administrators, including supervisors, principals, and superintendents and perhaps even to attorneys-at-law who might have occasion to be involved in a lawsuit involving a pupil injured in a school shop. It is intended to cover those phases of legal liability which directly affect teachers. Until recently, industrial education teachers have regarded these principles of legal liability with a degree of indifference bordering on complacency.

The material in this book is presented in a manner conducive to use in teacher education. Review questions and summaries have been especially prepared for this purpose. The main issues examined essentially pertain to public school teachers although it is acknowledged that a teacher in a private school or college could be involved in a legal action resulting from a pupil injury. While the same problem exists in private schools, it was concluded that this is a subject for another treatise.

It is a pleasure to recognize and acknowledge the contribution of others toward the completion of this project. Although the list of individuals is too long to reproduce here, those persons deserving special recognition include: Larry McMullen, attorney-at-law, Kansas City, Missouri, for his valuable contribution in pointing out some of the vagaries of legal research and assistance in locating pertinent court cases; Robert Sheran, Chief Justice, Minnesota Supreme Court, who provided the first introduction to the legal community; James F. Greenstein, attorney-at-law, St. Paul, Minnesota, for his counsel, suggestions, and legal analysis of the material; and Dr. H. H. London, professor emeritis of industrial education, University of Missouri, for his constructive crticism and able guidance.

Denis J. Kigin
Tempe, Arizona

Contents

CHAPTER 1

The Significance of Teacher Liability

THE possibility of a public school teacher being involved in a legal action resulting from a school-related injury is greater today than in any period of educational history. The problem is real! It must be faced directly and intelligently if teachers are to be protected from the financial burden and the ignominy of being a defendant in a court trial.

Doubt still exists in the minds of many teachers and administrators as to where their rights and responsibilities begin and end. Life today is almost impossible without the use of tools and machines, so consideration must be given to the legal and moral responsibilities of teaching potentially hazardous manipulative work. Numerous teachers have been involved in liability suits resulting from accidents in the school shop. In some instances they have been absolved of any negligence, but in others they have been held liable. An understanding of the teacher's potential liability in the event of pupil injury would assist in lessening the number of incidents resulting in court cases.

The intent of this book is to kindle an interest in the problem of shop-teacher liability and to identify certain needs which, as yet, have not been adequately met by existing laws and statutes. It is an attempt to gain the attention of some teachers and perhaps prevent them from facing a civil jury and wondering whether or not the verdict would hold them pecuniarily liable for negligence or failure to act. Attention will be given to procedures that may assist in preventing teachers from being involved in litigation when a major injury occurs in the school shop. The extent to which a shop teacher can be held liable in court actions under existing laws will be pointed out. An attempt will be made to clarify the extent of legal protection a teacher may enjoy in given states under certain conditions and to point out the possibility of preventing financial loss in case of an unfavorable court decision.

Basic Legal Considerations

A fundamental law governing the association of the teacher and pupils requires the avoidance of negligent conduct which might produce harm and injury to the pupils. The pupils have a reciprocal duty to be vigilant for their own protection in harmony with their age and maturity level. If an accident does occur and results in injury to a pupil, the teacher runs a calculated risk that it may terminate in a court action. Whether or not it will result in litigation is contingent on the actual circumstances leading up to the accident, or what was or was not done after the accident occurred.

The desire of a parent to seek damages for an injured pupil can well be understood. The desire of teachers to seek protection against such contingencies can also be appreciated. It may seem unfair for an injured pupil not to receive any compensation and it may be equally unfair to saddle the teacher with full responsibility for the injuries. Some injuries are entirely accidental which means, in effect, that the accident itself was unforeseeable, unavoidable, and that no one was to blame. This type of accident is normally referred to as a "pure accident" and no damages are recoverable. The process of elimination is often used in determining a "pure accident." When the known rules do not classify an injury as having occurred through the negligence or intentional wrongdoing of another, the accident is said to have been a "pure accident."

Difficulty often arises in distinguishing between an unavoidable or pure accident and one that results from negligence. A court will normally give full consideration to the possibility of some human failings or inadequacies before ruling that an accident was beyond the power of the teacher to prevent.

Terminology

Descriptive terms which are not common in everyday conversation are used in any treatise relating to the field of law. The terms themselves are legal in nature and are understood by those in the practice of law but frequently misunderstood by others. Many legal terms are used in this book, but an attempt has been made to accompany them with a definition which will be reasonably clear to those not familiar with legal terminology. The legal principles are stated in common language rather than in technical legalisms. In general, the terms have been given a broad, liberal meaning(*1*).

The term "school shop" is used throughout to describe all phases of industrial education, including industrial arts, technical, and vocational-industrial education. This is to facilitate meaning for those who are not acquainted with the evolution of terminology in the field of industrial education. The term "manual training" is used only when it is included in a ruling by a court or in a direct quotation. In the analyses of recorded court cases, it is next to impossible to distinguish between industrial-arts teachers and vocational-industrial teachers as separate categories. The general term "shop teacher" was adopted as an all-inclusive term identifying all teachers of shop subjects.

Limitations

The legal principles surrounding any aspect of liability are extensive and must be delimited in application to a specific area. Emphasis here is on the direct liability of teachers for pupil accidents in public school shops. However, the principles of law involved would be applicable to any other phase of the public educational system where pupil injuries might arise. The cases of court record reviewed are concerned primarily with public secondary schools involving actual shop-teacher liability or directly relating to shop-teacher liability. Cases involving school district liability were included for their informational and background value as they relate directly to phases of teacher liability.

Although shop-teacher responsibility on a scheduled field trip may justly fall within the scope of assigned duties, it is considered a major problem in itself and too broad to be included here. Also not included are related problems involving specific aspects of their own, such as those dealing with substitute teachers, student practice-teachers, and corporal punishment of pupils in the maintenance of discipline. Courts of individual states place their own demands on standards in these areas.

Case-Study Method

The citations reviewed are based on the National Reporter System, which is published by the West Publishing Company of St. Paul, Minnesota. It includes all cases of court record in all of the states. In order to become a case of court record, the case must reach the appellate or highest court of a state and a decision must be rendered. The system is divided

---

(*1*) See Glossary, Appendix A, p. 135.

into seven geographical sections (Atlantic, Northeastern, Southeastern, Southern, Southwestern, Pacific, and Northwestern) and includes all cases of court record from the assigned states in each section. In addition, the National Reporter System includes the *Supreme Court Reporter*, the *Federal Reporter*, and the *Federal Supplement*. New York State is reported in the *Northeastern Reporter* as well as in the *New York Supplement*.

The National Reporter System consists of two sets of volumes, an initial series and a second series, in each of the geographic sections, the *Federal Reporter*, and the *New York Supplement*. The *Federal Supplement*, first introduced in 1933, continues as a single series without interruption. The first volume of the *Northwestern Reporter* appeared in print in 1879, followed by the *Federal Reporter* in 1880, and the *Pacific Reporter* in 1884. The *Federal Reporter* was the first to inaugurate a second series in 1925, the *Southwestern Reporter* was next in 1928, and the *Pacific Reporter* followed in 1931. Other sections made the transition from the initial series to the second series without precedent, but with the number of reported cases as the prime mover.

Volumes in each series are in chronological order and are identified by number. The first volume in each series is number 1. The second series is clearly distinguished by the addition of "2d" in the title. Where appropriate, the "2d" is contained in case citations. Examples of how cases of record may be located from footnote citations are as follows:

Citation A: *Swanson* v. *School District No. 15 Pierce County,* 187 P. 386. Washington 1920.

Translation: Swanson is the plaintiff and School District No. 15 Pierce County is the defendant. A review of the pertinent facts of this case will be found in Volume 187 of the Pacific geographic section, initial series, on page 386 of the National Reporter System. This case was brought to trial in the State of Washington in 1920.

Citation B: *Miles* v. *School District No. 138 of Cheyenne County,* 281 N.W.2d 396. Nebraska 1979.

Translation: Miles is the plaintiff and School District No. 138 of Cheyenne County is the defendant. Relevant facts and court proceedings concerning this case are contained in Volume 281 of the Northwestern geographic section, *2nd series*, on page 396 of the National Reporter System. This case was brought to a conclusion in Nebraska in 1979.

It should be noted that the basic difference between Citations A and B is the addition of "2d" in Citation B. The 2d clearly establishes the second series as the basic source of information concerning the case under consideration.

Environment of the School Shop

The growth and expansion of the curriculum in the public schools have created problems which have added to the complexity of teaching. One of these problems involves the number and character of the activities generally accepted as a part of the industrial education program now included in the curriculum of a modern high school. The expanded offerings are so comprehensive that pupil participation adds significantly to the responsibilities of the teacher.

The use of tools and machines which are relatively hazardous to operate has accompanied the growth and expansion of the curriculum. A teacher, therefore, must be better prepared and more aware of his responsibilities to the pupils and the community than ever before.

Although approximately 60 percent of the cases presented as illustrations involve stationary power tools or machines, there are other considerations worthy of note. Hand tools have been a part of the process since the advent of the "manual training" movement. Improper use can result in injury, but usually of a secondary nature. The increased use of portable power tools in the school shop has not been without incident and has added another dimension to the potential for student injuries. These tools should be reserved for use by more mature and experienced students. The teacher has a continuing obligation to make the learning process safe. Despite precautions, however, accidents in the school shop are inevitable and some of these will result in litigation involving the teacher.

The place where a pupil engages in shop activity must be conducive to modern learning. Responsibility for providing a suitable place is shared by the school district and the teacher. The school district is required to provide adequate facilities and the teacher is expected to utilize them in a safe and proper manner. This dual responsibility of the school district and the teacher can perhaps best be summed up in the three "E's" of safety education. These are engineering, education, and enforcement.

Engineering

Engineering concerns itself primarily with the control of physical conditions, beginning with the building itself and including safety features that are a part of the overall design and function. The school district has the responsibility for providing a work area that is safe and healthy for pupils. The type of structure suitable for a school shop has unique features which are not necessary in an academic or lecture classroom. The teacher becomes involved in the engineering aspects of safety in the utilization and maintenance of the facilities provided. He may also assist in the planning and equipping of a new shop or the renovation of an existing structure.

Faulty shop conditions and equipment may lead to accidents. A building with a low ceiling and poor lighting may in itself be a factor in causing accidents. Unsuitable location of machines, which causes interference between operators, and failure to mark safety zones around machines may contribute to the accident totals. Poor construction of stock and supply facilities and lack of proper ventilation may be detrimental to the efficient and safe operation of a school shop.

Only tools and machines which are sanctioned by the school district belong in the shop. The teacher takes a calculated risk when he provides personal equipment for the pupils to use. Before doing so, the teacher must get written authorization from the administration, otherwise possible legal implications could constitute a serious problem.

Conditions which hinder the learning process and are actually a menace to the health and welfare of pupils should be remedied at the first opportunity. The teacher has an obligation to correct the conditions or to make recommendations in writing to the school administration for correction. Changes take time and money, but when they are for the betterment of education and the welfare of the pupils, they are well worth the investment.

Education

The teacher is the central figure in educating pupils to work safely. He also bears the brunt of the criticism should an accident occur. The method by which pupils can best be taught safe work habits in the shop may differ with the individual situation and the age and maturity level of the pupils. It may also depend on the type of class, school policies, and the qualifications and experience of the teacher.

In the process of educating for safety, regardless of the method used, it is well to remember that secondary-school pupils have become accustomed to being deluged with rules and regulations. Rules and regulations governing the activities in the school shop must, therefore, be clearly stated and made meaningful. The pupils must develop a thorough understanding of their purpose and be made to see how they, as individuals, can benefit by observing them.

The responsibility of the teacher to teach the pupils the necessary rules of safety is evident. A positive approach has been found most successful in accomplishing this. Pupils learn best through experience, both real and vicarious, and it is up to the teacher to provide it. The experiences should be integrated throughout the entire course of study, rather than as a separate course or unit within a course. The pupil should receive positive instructions, not negative warnings.

Enforcement

One of the most important features of successful accident prevention is enforcement of safety rules, which means insistence that the rules and regulations be followed consistently and completely. In the school shop, this responsibility rests squarely on the shoulders of the teacher. Unfortunately, it is frequently taken lightly because of complacency or apathy on the part of the teacher. The danger is enhanced by the feeling: if all has been going well, why get excited? Such teachers may just be lucky in avoiding serious injury and possible litigation.

The general rules pertaining to the overall operation of the school usually contain a degree of flexibility. Whether or not an individual will be penalized for a violation of these rules depends on several factors, such as the temperament of the disciplinarian and whether or not the individual was caught in the infraction. This does not hold true with power machinery; the important rules governing their operations are not arbitrary. They are absolute and allow no irregularity in their enforcement. The machine is an inanimate object and has no consideration for inexperience or momentary carelessness.

Pupils are always watching, studying, and imitating the actions of the teacher. If a teacher performs a particular operation in a dangerous manner, the pupils will assume that this is an acceptable way to do it. Enforcement of safety regulations can be enhanced with the addition of another "E," representing "example." The teacher must provide a consistently good example for all pupils in his class at all times.

Too many teachers feel that imparting safety information to the pupils the first week or so of class consummates their duty. It is often done halfheartedly as though they themselves are not convinced of its importance. They perform this haphazard service just to meet the minimum requirements. This is not sufficient! Pupils must constantly be reminded of the potential hazards inherent in working with tools and machines. They can acquire the desire and the ability to protect themselves from potential danger through a well-organized and regulated program. This can only be accomplished by a teacher who is enthusiastic about safe procedures. A fifth "E," for "enthusiasm," can be added, making a total of five "E's" describing the teacher's role in accident prevention.

The Possibility of Liability

Periodically, interest is aroused by a liability case of state or national importance involving a school pupil. Cases of this magnitude have made educators aware of the likelihood of liability and its related effects. Teachers must be informed of how the doctrine of legal liability affects them in their everyday school activities. They should be cognizant of the basic legal principles governing their profession. They should have a working knowledge of the statutory enactments and significant court decisions which directly affect the operation of the state systems of education and be familiar with where this information can be obtained. These constitute some of the working tools of a well-informed professional educator, whether teacher or administrator.

The principles of liability apply equally to all teachers, regardless of what they teach. But a realization of the potential dangers involved should not in any way restrain a teacher from teaching well. The intent here is not to frighten or discourage potential teachers from teaching shop subjects but to enlighten them so that they will be able to do a more competent job of teaching.

The number of court actions resulting from school-related pupil injuries has increased in recent years. Reasons for this increase are closely associated with the expanding school program, greater awareness of the possibility of successful court actions, and changes in state laws.

All accidents occurring in the school shop involving pupil injury do not result in litigation. From a legal standpoint, an analysis of those accidents which do not result in litigation is important, primarily to establish what conditions were prevalent at the time of the accident and possible reasons why they are not litigated.

The type of machine or equipment on which a pupil is injured has no significant effect on the extent of teacher liability. However, the extent of a pupil's injury often influences the amount of damages recoverable. Fortunately, the view that every person should be held responsible for his or her wrongful conduct is fundamental in our society. The law imposes penalties only on those whose wrongful acts succeed in causing damage or injury to other persons and property.

CHAPTER 2

Elements of Liability

CERTAIN factors relate to the establishment of teacher liability and provide a basis for understanding this phase of law. Liability here is broadly defined as the state of being responsible by law for damages stemming from pupil injuries. The elements which contribute to a teacher's liability or provide the foundation for avoiding legal entanglements must be clearly identified and examined.

Many classroom teachers and administrators regard legal principles applicable to public education with apathy or disinterest. This may be conditioned by the fact that they do not believe it is within the realm of their duties to be concerned with this aspect of education. This does not mean that regulations are disregarded intentionally, rather that they are probably overlooked through a lack of knowledge and understanding of school laws and rules.

Court records indicate that on occasion individual teachers have been called on to defend themselves in cases involving pupil injury. The injured pupil and his or her parents have the legal right of redress in money damages for injuries incurred in connection with any school activity. Since the restoration of a lost eye, arm, finger, or leg, or the reactivation of an impaired organ of the body is impossible, the law seeks to compensate to a degree with a monetary consideration.

Parents of injured pupils may also institute court action for reimbursement of the cost of medical services. In the case of a fatal accident, they may file suit for the wrongful death of a pupil. According to the law, the parents of a pupil who is fatally injured or who is permanently crippled in an accident caused by negligence are entitled to damages based on the potential earnings of the child. If that pupil's earning capacity is lessened or destroyed by the accident, the parents themselves are injured economically.

Pupils are minors, so they are not permitted to sue on their own behalf. Parents or guardians, as representatives of an injured pupil, may use a variety of legal attacks including a multiple suit. The individual teacher or the school district may be named as the defendant. In some situations the teacher and the school district may be named as codefendants.

Theory of Liability

Pupils, attending modern, well-equipped public schools, are expected to participate in a wide range of activities. Without question, these opportunities have intensified the pupils' broad learning experiences. At the same time they have increased the possibility of injury through a closer proximity to hazards. School shops and laboratories contain equipment and materials which are potentially hazardous. This equipment has become as much a necessity in most schools as any of the common items which constitute a well-furnished classroom.

The shop teacher assumes a degree of responsibility for the welfare and safety of the pupils in his charge by virtue of his assigned duties. Any deviation from the normal supervision required of a teacher may result in his being held liable for any injury that may result. Because of the nature of the activities which are a normal part of the industrial-education curriculum, the shop teacher is placed in a rather precarious position.

A teacher in charge of a school shop is expected to supervise the pupils more closely than would be necessary in the lecture/discussion-type classroom. The youth and inexperience of the pupils increase the precautions necessary to minimize risk. The teacher has the prime responsibility for regularly inspecting facilities and equipment to correct potential hazards before allowing the pupils to use them. A teacher who does not instruct a pupil on the proper method of using a tool or power machine or does not supervise to see that proper procedures are followed is omitting a specific legal duty. If an injury results, the teacher may be declared negligent and, thereby, liable for tort. A tort is a type of legal action putting into effect the principle of law that stipulates that injured parties have recourse against those who have caused them injury.

Teachers cannot guarantee that no injuries or damages will result from their acts, nor is this expected of them. In general, claims against school employees will be sustained in court only if it can be shown that injury to a pupil occurred because the employees had exceeded their authority, used poor judgment, were negligent, or failed to take reasonable precautions.

In the event of an accident in a school shop, the nature of the accident and the place where it occurred may determine whether the school district, the individual teacher, or both are liable. Although it may be found in some instances that the apparent cause of an accident was carelessness on the part of the pupil, the basic responsibility could rest with the teacher, or even with the school administration, through failure to provide proper equipment, supervision, or instruction.

Whenever an accident occurs in the school causing personal injury to a pupil, one of the first inquiries following the comforting of the injured has to do with who was to blame. A corollary question usually consists of what caused the accident and could it have been prevented? Perhaps one of the most realistic problems following an accident of this sort is basically economic, establishing who will be expected to pay for any necessary medical expenses and possible hospitalization.

Many factors must be considered in establishing what legal liability really is and its effect on the individual shop teacher. In the event of a school accident in which a pupil sustains personal injuries, there is usually a combination of events which may or may not lead to a teacher's liability, and each event must be considered individually and on its own merits. These events are those which are directly related to the conditions surrounding the accident. If the facts absolve the teacher of negligence, he will not be held liable. The assumption is, then, that negligence is the key factor in determining liability.

The school district as well as the teacher can be legally liable. The corporate liability of a school district depends on whether or not: (1) the statutes of the state are silent, (2) existing state statues preserve the school district's governmental immunity, (3) existing state statutes or court decisions abrogate the school district's governmental immunity, or (4) existing statutes impose liability. In the absence of a statute, tort liability rests on common-law principles. Common law is the law that was in force in England at the time the United States was formed and remains the law unless changed for a particular state by legislation (see chapter 3).

Liability is established where there is proof of negligence. Tort liability, as defined for this purpose, is dependent on the negligence of the individual who is the legal cause of the injury. The meaning of negligence and the points of law concerning liability for negligent acts that cause injury, therefore, must be thoroughly examined.

Negligence

However reasonable the actions of a teacher may seem, they frequently create a risk for one or more of the pupils. These actions could be termed negligent if the risks involved are unreasonably great and are prone to cause undue harm. Some situations require a greater degree of care than do others because the hazards are greater. What constitutes negligence is a question of fact in all cases with a jury determining whether or not the acts complained of are negligent.

An intentional act is not negligence. Negligence in a truly defined sense is unintentional. There are certain basic elements which are necessary for an action based on negligence.

1. Primary among these elements is the *failure of the individual to act so as to protect others from unnecessary risks.* When such failure results in injury to another causing loss or damages, it could result in the charge of negligence.

2. *Negligence also consists of the failure to act as a reasonably prudent and careful person would under the circumstances involved.* An analysis of this definition would indicate that either action or inaction may constitute negligence. Negligence thereby becomes a factual question with the specific events surrounding an incident being of utmost importance. The shop teacher's assigned duties normally indicate what may or may not be expected of him, with the resultant implications for negligence.

3. Negligence has also been defined in the popular sense as *lack of due diligence or care*. This, applied to the shop teacher, could involve such things as care of the physical facilities, care and maintenance of tools and equipment, adequate supervision, safety instruction, and proper example. Negligence can, therefore, be interpreted as substandard conduct as compared to the standard contained in the law for the protection of pupils against unreasonable risk of injury.

4. It can also be considered negligent to *permit a third person* (person other than the teacher or the pupil) *to use an object or to engage in an activity* if the teacher knows, or should know, that the person is likely to use the object or to conduct himself in the activity in such a manner as to create an unreasonable risk of harm to himself or others.

The final judgment of who is negligent and under what specific conditions is difficult to predetermine. Negligence is usually determined by a group of laymen who compose a civil jury and not by professional educators. In a broad sense, there are three main groups of people who might be held liable in a school accident once negligence has been proved. These groups would include the board of education, the school administrators, and the individual teacher. Unless governmental immunity has been abrogated, the board of education of a school district, as a governmental agency, is not liable for accidents occurring in connection with school activities. It is also extremely rare for a school administrator to be held negligent because the administrator is not personally liable for the negligent performance of teachers who are expected to exercise discretion or judgment in the performance of their official functions. However, the teacher does not enjoy the same exemption from liability as does the employing school board.

From a critical analysis of these three groups, it is evident that the teacher is in a vulnerable position. The teacher could be termed liable if his negligent conduct is the legal cause of the harm suffered by another. The legal cause of an injury is that cause without which the pupil would not have been injured and which, in the natural sequence of events, produced the resultant harm. When the teacher's conduct is a substantial factor in bringing about the harm, and if there is no rule of law relieving him of liability, there can be little doubt as to where the responsibility lies.

Involved in the determination of fault following an accident is the principle of *res ipsa loquitur*, which means that the act or thing speaks for itself. If the evidence shows that the injury could have resulted only through the negligence of the teacher even though it occurred in such a way that the injured pupil cannot prove how it happened, the principle of *res ipsa loquitur* would apply.

Interpretations of the law by courts and other legal authorities indicate that a teacher is governed by the common-law obligation that every person must act or use that which he controls so as not to injure another. Where situations or conditions of possible danger exist, anticipation of this danger must be recognized and the teacher must assume the responsibility for the protection of the pupils from this potential danger. Self-injury by pupils as a result of childish acts, immaturity, or irresponsibility is a possibility and teachers have the duty to protect the pupils against themselves. A very high degree of care in supervision is required if the teacher is to avoid the charge of negligence. In this regard, a teacher can be considered negligent if his actions in the classroom are not for the educational benefit of pupils.

Failure to anticipate and report conditions which are hazardous may place undue responsibilities on the teacher. Negligence is then to be gauged by the ability to anticipate danger and the consequences of dangerous conditions. The scope of his authority regulates the character of his obligations and, therefore, regulates the kind of conduct necessary to avoid the charge of negligence.

Conditions, circumstances, and often physical surroundings combine in the assessment of negligence. In *Maxwell* v. *Santa Fe Public Schools*(1) action was brought by a student following an eye injury sustained when a glass container exploded in a science class. The question of negligence was held for the jury in *Bottorf* v. *Waltz*(2). The plaintiff, Bottorf, charged the defendant, an art teacher, with negligence when a makeshift mold fell and spilled melted wax on the student's back. In *Bush* v. *Oscoda Area Schools*(3) a fourteen-year-old girl was severely injured when a container of wood alcohol exploded in a physical science class. The class was held in a classroom designated for mathematics but without modification for science equipment. A negligent action charge was brought against the teacher, the principal, the superintendent, and the school district.

Shop teachers are expected to conduct themselves in a careful manner to avoid negligence. This does not imply that they are to have the pupils avoid all situations in which they could be injured. It does mean, however, that they are to use a high degree of care under such circumstances. Parents, professional educators, and school administrators must accept the premise that it is unrealistic to shield pupils from all possible situations in which injury may occur.

In reality, there is no rule of thumb for determining what is negligent action and what is not. Although each individual case is decided on its own merits, there are certain common conditions under which a teacher is more likely to be considered negligent should an accident occur. Perhaps one of the most significant of these conditions is absence of the teacher from the classroom while the class is in session. Other conditions of particular importance include neglect of equipment, lack of proper safety instructions, lack of due care with regard to the age and maturity of the pupils, and lack of insistence that proper safeguards be used.

American laws of negligence are based on the theory of precedent, previous judicial decisions, or established modes of legal procedures. The fact that an accident occurs and the teacher is negligent does not always mean that he is liable for damages. It must be proved that the negligence is reasonably connected with the resultant injury before the negligent person may be held liable.

The law contains a series of defenses for those charged with negligence as a result of which even a negligent person may escape liability for his

---

(1) *Maxwell* v. *Sante Fe Public Schools,* 534 P.2d 307. New Mexico 1975.

(2) *Bottorf* v. *Waltz,* 369 A.2d 332. Pennsylvania 1976.

(3) *Bush* v. *Oscoda Area Schools,* 250 N.W.2d 759. Michigan 1977.

negligence under certain circumstances. First of all, the negligence must have some substantial connection with the injury complained of. In addition, the pupils themselves must refrain from being negligent with respect to their own welfare. This means, in part, that it is possible that contributory negligence on the part of the injured party could cancel out the teacher's negligence.

Contributory Negligence

The final assessment of responsibility for injuries sustained as a result of a school-shop accident may hinge on the actions of the pupil with regard to his or her own personal safety. If the pupil has failed to act with reasonable prudence, it may be said that he was contributorily negligent. Contributory negligence involves the plaintiff's failure to care for personal safety, which, in effect, means that the pupil's own negligent action contributed to the resultant injury. It can relieve the teacher of liability for any concurrent negligence on his part unless the judge or jury takes the age and maturity level of the injured pupil into consideration. Realistically, the defense of contributory negligence is often of little value when a minor is involved.

The determining or assigning of the responsibility of contributory negligence is complicated by the realization that minors are not expected to use the same degree of care as adults. Reasonable self-protection is expected of all mentally and physically sound adults, but courts do not employ adult standards when considering the possibility of a pupil's contributory negligence. The courts are more prone to consider the pupil's age and the negligent act commensurate with that degree of care which would be determined as standard for average children of a similar age group.

The teacher of adolescents is presumed to know the vagaries of the minds of pupils, and is expected to anticipate their actions and shield the students from unexpected difficulties by direct supervision. In reality, the individual teacher is not actually responsible for what happens to the pupil, but is responsible for the reasonable consequences of negligence with regard to the pupil. A pupil's age may be a factor in determining the teacher's breach of duty in cases where the pupil is too young to be charged with contributory negligence. It might be expected that even though the pupil realizes that his act is dangerous, he or she is not capable of knowing the full extent of the danger. For example, it might be said that even though a pupil knows that there is danger in using a power machine without a guard, he or she is not aware of the amount of the danger. The use of the machine under hazardous circumstances does not constitute contributory negligence. The responsibility here reverts to the teacher and the school district for allowing an unguarded machine to be used.

The determination of contributory negligence normally bars any recovery on the part of the plaintiff. This is true in all states where the courts have not yet taken the responsibility of apportioning the degree of fault between the defendant and the plaintiff.

Comparative Negligence

A more recent concept relating to contributory negligence that has gained noteworthy acceptance is the principle of comparative negligence. In the application of this principle, the courts assign the degree of fault between the defendant and the plaintiff and apportion the amount of the recovery possible for the plaintiff. The doctrine of comparative negligence has been in effect in Oregon since 1911. The Oregon statute provides that the contributory negligence of the person injured shall not be a defense, but may be taken into account by the jury in fixing the amount of the damage.

Comparative negligence has been looked on with favor by many because recovery is diminished in proportion to the extent to which the injury was caused by the plaintiff's own negligence. This apportionment of damages differs from the traditional concept of contributory negligence in which no recovery is possible.

Comparative negligence is regarded as more equitable for both sides in a controversy if it is properly safeguarded. Recovery is possible in proportion to the extent to which the injury was caused by the defendant's own negligence, or in so far as his negligence exceeds that of the plaintiff. In theory, if the assigned negligence is 50 percent for the plaintiff and 50 percent for the defendant, there would be no recovery.

More than 25 states have statutes which call for the apportionment of damages in certain cases. Not all of these states are in agreement as to the degree of apportionment, or the method used in the determination of the combined negligence. There are several states which have statutes of general application, while Tennessee has adopted the principle as a matter of common law. In the states of Arkansas and Mississippi, damages will be apportioned even though the plaintiff is more negligent than the defendant. Two other states, Georgia and Wisconsin, apportion damages only when the plaintiff's negligence is less than the defendant's. Nebraska and South Dakota courts are prone to apply the principle only where the plaintiff's negligence is slight in comparison with the defendant's established negligence, and the state of Tennessee uses the principle in cases in which the plaintiff's negligence is only a remote cause of the injury.

As has been noted, the procedure for the apportionment of damages under comparative negligence differs in individual states. An argument that has been brought out against the adoption of comparative negligence is that juries are not capable of weighing relative negligence or of determining accurately the proportions of negligence of the litigants. Another objection is that insurance premiums would rise, since insurance companies would be responsible for payment of damages in many instances where they now pay nothing under the rule of contributory negligence.

Proximate Cause

Proximate cause is the direct or immediate cause of the resultant injury to the pupil. A shop teacher can be held liable for injuries sustained by a pupil in a school shop if the negligent action of the teacher is found to be the direct cause of the injury. There must be a decision as to whether or not the careless conduct of the teacher was a substantial factor in causing the injury and whether or not the careless conduct was the direct cause of the injury. In line with this reasoning, it is possible for a teacher to be negligent and still not be held liable for damages, providing the negligence complained of was not the proximate or direct cause of the injury. However, failure to plan for probable consequences may be the proximate cause of an injury to a pupil.

In *Ohman* v. *Board of Education of New York*(4), proximate cause was a prominent feature. The board of education was absolved of liability even though the circumstances surrounding the incident included the established fact that the teacher was out of the classroom when the injury occurred. The court, in ruling on this case, said that it did not follow that absence from the classroom by the teacher was the proximate or injury-producing cause. They ruled that the injury was caused by the act of a third party (another student) throwing a drafting pencil. The court ruled further that the injury could have occurred while the teacher was in the classroom, and that a drawing pencil was not classified as a dangerous instrument.

The *Ohman* case has left its mark in the annals of school law. A 3-2 decision for the defendant school district was rendered in 1949 by the New York Court of Appeals. The principles derived from this case have been applied to every succeeding case where a student injury occurred during

(4) *Ohman* v. *Board of Education of New York*, 90 N.E.2d 474. New York 1949.

the teacher's absence from the classroom. The decision has drawn severe criticism from educators and the courts alike. Dissenters and other authorities argued that absence from the classroom had the effect of lessening discipline and heightened the possibility of horseplay. They also reasoned that an event such as this could be foreseen by a teacher and that a sharp pencil could be dangerous.

The dissenting judges in the *Ohman* case made the statement that: "Children have a known proclivity to act impulsively without thought of the possibilities of danger. It is precisely this lack of mature judgment which makes supervision so vital. The mere presence of the hand of authority and discipline normally is effective to curb this youthful exuberance and to protect children against their own folly."

The *Ohman* decision continues to have an effect on cases based on proximate cause and the presence or absence of the teacher from the classroom. In *Butler* v. *District of Columbia*(5), the court concluded that the teacher's absence from the classroom did not establish liability for negligence on the part of school authorities. A junior-high-school student lost the sight of one eye when hit in the eye by a flying object, presumably a piece of type, as he entered the print shop. The suit alleged that school authorities were negligent in supervision of the classroom and that their negligence constituted the proximate cause of the injury. The teacher had been assigned to duty as hall and cafeteria supervisor under a plan formulated by the principal of the school. Students in the printing class were provided specific rules of conduct to be observed if the teacher was not present. One rule was that students were "not to throw type." In ruling for the defendant school district, the court stated that the rules of conduct balanced the need for a teacher to supervise several hundred students in the corridors and cafeteria against the need to supervise 14 students in a classroom for a short period. The teacher arrived in the classroom 12 minutes after the class was to start.

Alleged proximate cause on the part of an injured student was the deciding factor in *Miles* v. *School District #138 of Cheyenne County*(6). Injuries sustained by a 17-year-old student resulted in a charge of negligence leveled against the school district for the manner in which the woodshop class was conducted. The student had attempted to remove a piece of wood from the jointer while it was running, thereby injuring her right hand and suffering the loss of two fingers. The court determined that by

---

(5) *Butler* v. *District of Columbia,* 417 F.2d 1150. District of Columbia 1969.

(6) *Miles* v. *School District #138 of Cheyenne County,* 281 N.W. 396. Nebraska 1979.

reason of instruction given, demonstrations performed, and over one year of experience in the safe and proper operation of the jointer, the student was thoroughly familiar with its operation and the hazards attendant thereto. In ruling in favor of the defendant school district, the court held that the student's negligence in placing her left hand in the rotating blades of the jointer was the sole proximate cause of the injury she sustained in the unfortunate accident.

In another court case(7) reviewed from the National Reporter System, the absence of proximate cause was an important factor in relieving a teacher of liability. Action was brought against a teacher of industrial arts in a public school for injuries sustained by a pupil in his class. The injuries occurred while the pupil, at the direction of the teacher, was cleaning a hand printing press. A fellow student moved the fly wheel on the press and the pupil's hand was caught in the gears. The court granted a motion for nonsuit on the ground that the act of a fellow pupil in moving the fly wheel of the press was the proximate or direct cause of the accident, breaking the chain of causation between the accident and any conduct on the part of the teacher. The teacher, therefore, was held not liable.

Courts have ruled, as in the case above, that negligent acts of fellow students are independent intervening causes which break the chain of causation between the accident and the asserted negligence of the defendant and thereby become the proximate cause of the accident. An intervening cause may be defined as one which produces the resultant injury, taking place after the teacher's negligent act occurred. But care must be taken with this principle because the conduct on the part of the third person must be extraordinary and unforeseeable before it can be said that it is the superseding cause of harm. The qualities of these intervening causes are technical in nature and depend on the interpretation of a jury. It must be emphasized that in order to relieve the teacher of liability, the intervening cause must not have been foreseen by him, nor can the intervening cause be a reaction from the risk originally created by the defendant.

Foreseeability

It is very important for individuals involved in school work to attempt painstakingly to identify all possible risks and to take immediate precautionary steps to alleviate these risks, since foreseeability of hazards is a basic issue in most liability cases. It has been alleged that the first test to

---

(7) *Taylor* v. *Kevlin,* 1 A.2d 433. New Jersey 1938.

determine whether or not there has been negligence is the test of foreseeability. The question then becomes: What should a reasonably prudent shop teacher foresee as unsafe conditions in the school shop and what are the possible consequences that might result from unsafe conditions? This immediately involves safety devices and their condition, hand tools and their condition, and power tools and their condition. In addition, it includes safety practices and encompasses the entire safety program of the shop teacher. The key to the determination of reasonably prudent action is to be gauged by the ability of the teacher to anticipate or to foresee danger. Prevention can best be achieved by careful attention to the focal points of trouble.

It is difficult to ascertain at what point or stage of operation a tool or power machine becomes dangerous and what specific conditions must be present to make it so. The shop teacher must, therefore, prudently teach the necessary safety rules and practices, since pupils in most school-shop classes are called on to operate potentially hazardous machinery. Tools and machines are inanimate objects, so it must be assumed that they cannot be classified as dangerous in themselves. Considering this basic premise, it can be said that there is no such thing as a dangerous tool. Tools and machines then become only as safe or as unsafe as the operator and the hands that guide them.

It is the responsibility of the individual teacher to see that tools and machines are used in a correct and safe manner and are not pushed beyond their limitations. From the standpoint of safety and the physical welfare of the pupils, it is the duty of the teacher to anticipate danger or an accident and to remove the circumstances which may cause an accident. Should the shop teacher fail to act, he is negligent by reason of omission rather than commission, which can be interpreted as lack of foreseeability. In addition, and from the standpoint of legal liability, the teacher should also be able to perceive the consequences of an accident. This means, then, that it is important for a shop teacher not only to foresee possible dangerous situations, but also to be aware of the consequences of a resultant accident should the dangerous condition be allowed to exist.

In *Lilienthal* v. *San Leandro Unified School District*(8), evidence was sufficient for the jury to declare the teacher negligent. However, the school district was held liable for the damages since California has abrogated the principle of common-law immunity and permits actions against

---

(8) *Lilienthal* v. *San Leandro Unified School District*, 298 P.2d 889 (California 1956).

school districts. Proceedings were instigated following an accident in which a pupil suffered permanent disability when a knife was deflected into his eye. The court ruled that there was sufficient evidence that the teacher should have foreseen the dangerous situation and that he was inattentive and careless in failing to observe and stop the action before the injury occurred. This case is discussed in more detail in Chapter 3.

From the above illustration it can be seen that the courts place great weight on the factor of foreseeability as related to liability. A teacher could be held guilty of negligence if he pursued a course of action not consistent with that of a reasonably prudent person with regard to the pupil's personal safety. It is not necessary that a teacher be able to foresee the *exact* nature of the injury or the degree of severity; it is enough if a reasonably prudent person could have foreseen that some kind of injury might have resulted from an action taken, or from an action that should have been taken but was not.

Foreseeability was a prominent consideration in the court deciding for the defendant teacher in *Morris* v. *Ortiz*(9). The plaintiff, Morris, suffered severe hand and finger cuts while a member of a group of students attempting to bend the top of a dismantled automobile. The plaintiff claimed the defendant teacher was negligent in allowing a member of the class to jump on the top unexpectedly while the plaintiff and others were holding it a few feet off the floor. The trial court directed a verdict for the defendant which was subsequently reversed by the Court of Appeals and ultimately upheld by the Arizona Supreme Court. The Supreme Court concluded that the act of the boy jumping on the auto top was "wholly unexpected" and that the teacher could not have forseen nor anticipated his action. One Supreme Court Judge dissented and took the position that the teacher was aware that his students had been jumping on the auto top before he told them they should "give up" and scrap the top.

In *Banks* v. *Seattle School District No. 1*(10), the principle of foreseeability was a factor in determining judgment for the plaintiff. In an action by a pupil against the school district for injuries sustained when the pupil's foot slipped while operating a printing press, negligence was charged on the part of the school district in failing to properly guard the printing press. Evidence that the district installed a guard on the foot treadle of the press following the accident was admissible, not as evidence

(9) *Morris* v. *Ortiz*, 437 P.2d 652. Arizona 1968. This case first cited under 415 P.2d 114 (Arizona 1966) and involved School District No. 1 of Pima County. Remanded for jury trial against the teacher.

(10) *Banks* v. *Seattle School District No. 1*, 80 P.2d 835. Washington 1938.

of past negligence, but to support the contention that it should have been foreseen that the press could be adequately guarded.

There are probably two ways in which the lack of foreseeability could affect the teacher's liability. In some states, such as Pennsylvania, it is held that the defendant's negligent act is the proximate cause of only the foreseeable consequences of an act. In some of the other states, such as New York, it is held that there is no obligation toward a plaintiff unless injury to the plaintiff could have been foreseen. Foreseeability is accepted as a common limitation to the defendant's liability. As such, obligation to the plaintiff would be determined by the judge with proximate cause as a question of fact for the jury. Both have the potential to influence the amount of liability.

The amount of care required of a teacher in a given situation is contingent on the total threatened danger. A condition which is allowed to exist in view of either the teacher's knowledge or his conscious ignorance is dangerous to the extent that there is a good chance of harm resulting from this condition. If the harm ultimately sustained varies greatly from what might have been foreseen, the conduct causing the harm is not considered negligent.

Assumption of Risk

Assumption of risk is a legal defense capable of negating liability through a person's voluntary participation in a hazardous situation with full knowledge of the dangers involved. Broadly interpreted, the principle of assumption of risk means in part that when a plaintiff accepts a very reasonable risk and fails to exercise proper care for his own safety, it may provide a defense available to the defendant. Assumption of risk thereby assumes knowledge of a danger and a conscious willingness on the part of an individual to participate regardless of the danger. This principle, as applied to teacher liability, would mean that the pupil is aware of the risk involved in the school shop and makes a voluntary choice to encounter it.

Although this principle may apply in some circumstances, courts are prone to apply it in special situations only. When an adult willingly participates in an activity involving certain risks of which he is aware, he cannot claim damages for any resulting injury. School pupils, however, are generally classified as minors and are not expected to possess the same degree of reasoning power that enables adults to determine the possible danger of certain activities. Historically, courts have ruled that the immaturity of students, the resultant inability to understand completely the consequences of their acts, and their lack of complete responsibility for their own behavior make them incapable of assuming a given risk.

More recently courts have granted teachers and school districts some relief in this area. In *Hutchinson* v. *Toews(11)*, knowledge of risk and contributory negligence precluded recovery from the teacher and school district for injury to a student sustained when a mixture of potassium chlorate and powdered sugar exploded prematurely. The court concluded from the evidence presented that the injured student had knowledge of the risk involved in the experiment and that he was contributorily negligent as a matter of law. Assumption of risk and contributory negligence as applied to tort liabilty were main areas of discussion in *Chase* v. *Shasta Lake Union School District(12)* and in *Arnold* v. *Hafling(13)*. In the latter case, the court ruled that since the students involved were 16 and 18 years of age, respectively, it would be expected that they would be more responsible than elementary school children.

In certain activities carried on in connection with our modern schools, a pupil must assume the normal exposure of participation. This is particularly true in school-shop classes where the very nature of the prescribed work necessitates the handling of industrial-type tools and the operation of power equipment. It is reasonable to assume that although some of the pupils injured in shop accidents were aware that a risk was involved, they lacked the experience to know how great the risk was. Under this supposition, the pupil cannot be said to have made a voluntary choice to encounter the risk actually involved.

The magnitude of the risk is an important factor, for when it is said that a pupil assumes some risk in a school shop, he does not assume the risk of defective equipment, incompetent instruction, or inadequate directions to accomplish some task beyond his capabilities. A review of court cases will substantiate the fact that the defense of assumption of risk is rarely successful in actions brought by an injured pupil against a teacher or a school district.

Although it can be expected that pupils take certain measures to protect themselves from perils that may constitute a menace, the teacher is required to give warning of its existence and otherwise guard against injury where peril has been discovered. The school district itself, which operates and maintains the physical facilities, owes the duty of freedom

---

(11) *Hutchinson* v. *Toews,* 476 P.2d 811. Oregon 1970.

(12) *Chase* v. *Shasta Lake Union School District,* 259 A.C.A (No. 3) 648. California 1968.

(13) *Arnold* v. *Hafling*. 474 P.2d 638. Colorado 1970.

from menace and peril in favor of the personnel who come into contact with these facilities.

Summary

Practically all legal actions against school districts or individual shop teachers resulting from injuries to pupils in school shops are based on negligence. Negligence, which is basic to the whole problem of liability and is defined as "the failure to exercise due care" under particular circumstances, must ordinarily be proved by the plaintiff with the burden of proof being on the plaintiff. Since juries composed of laymen usually determine liability in court cases, the actions of the shop teacher must bear the sign of common sense.

The public school system must be responsive to, and appreciative of, the general mores of the people. If a pupil is injured in a school-shop accident, it may be expected that someone may be held liable for damages. The school district in most instances is immune from liability in tort, but this immunity does not apply to the individual shop teacher, and he often becomes the logical defendant. This is true even though school teachers can be classified as state employees and, in the discharge of their duties, render services for a public purpose. It is important to realize that shop teachers may be sued and held liable for injuries suffered by pupils in class if negligence can be found to be the proximate or immediate cause.

Teachers can avoid most liability suits if they realize and accept the fact that the safety of the pupils under their control is their responsibility. In addition, pupils should be made aware that this is a cooperative venture in which they are the ultimate beneficiaries and a reciprocal duty is owed by them to be vigilant for their own protection. Pupils should be encouraged to point out malfunctioning equipment to the teacher and to refrain from attempting activities beyond their ability. It is also important to stress proper care for minor injuries and to recognize the rights and properties of others.

There are many specific conditions of a physical and human nature which must be properly controlled by the shop teacher in order to avoid being held legally liable for the injury of pupils in his shop. In deciding whether or not the teacher's act constituted negligence, the courts must consider several factors. The factual cause of an injury is usually obvious, but the legal cause is more complex and involves many subordinate elements. It can be said that an act is the legal cause of an injury when an individual disregards the foreseeable consequences which a reasonably prudent person could have foreseen as harmful. The measure of foreseeability is used as the first test in determining liability and whether or not the defendant's conduct was the legal cause of the plaintiff's injury.

Generally speaking, one is liable in a negligence suit if it can be shown that the injuries to another were the direct result of the improper actions of the defendant. Basically, this means that in order to hold a teacher responsible for an injury suffered by a pupil, there must be an unbroken connection between the wrongful act and the resultant injury. If the conduct of the teacher bears no reasonable connection with the harm done, he cannot be considered at fault.

It is assumed that pupils accept some reasonable risk involving school work within the limits of their age and maturity level. When they fail to exercise proper care for their own safety and an accident results, defenses of contributory negligence and assumption of risk may be available to the defendant. Contributory negligence involves a degree of deviation from the standard of conduct expected of the plaintiff and automatically destroys all claims of injured persons who have contributed to their own injuries, while assumption of risk assumes knowledge of the danger that may be inherent. In the application of the principles of contributory negligence and assumption of risk to pupils of school age, it may be unreasonable to assume that they are capable of understanding the complications of the dangers involved. From this it can be construed that these principles are rarely accepted by a jury as a defense for a teacher in a negligence action.

Contributory negligence along with assumption of risk are normally questions of fact for the jury, with the burden of proof on the defendant, whereas, the plaintiff has the burden of proof in the case of ordinary negligence. Only in the clearest cases will recovery be barred or denied on the ground that the plaintiff was contributorily negligent as a matter of law, particularly when a minor is involved. Mere pupil knowledge of the existence of danger will not necessarily bar recovery for injuries sustained by a pupil.

In determining whether or not contributory negligence and/or assumption of risk are valid defenses, extreme care should be used in assessing the conduct of a student of any age, tested against two basic premises: (1) whether there was gross disregard of safety in the face of known, perceived, and understood dangers; and (2) whether there was intentional exposure to obvious danger in connection with nontechnical and ordinary objects and situations within the capacity of the age and maturity level of the student to appreciate and realize. The age of the student involved has a direct effect on court decisions, but at the present time there is no magic number.

Comparative negligence is a modern evolution of contributory negligence and allows the payment of damages in proportion to the extent to which the injury was caused by the defendant's own negligence, but only in the situation where the defendant's negligence exceeds that of the plaintiff. This concept has been looked on by many as a fairer means of apportionment of damages because the plaintiff is allowed a percentage of recovery even when his negligence contributes to the accident or injuries.

Principles of negligence and liability are especially important to teachers connected with activities in which some danger is inherent. Shop teachers are in positions which expose them more frequently to charges of negligence for pupil injuries than are teachers of so-called academic subjects. In view of these facts, teachers will want to safeguard their pupils by taking all reasonable precautions against the possibility of harm. Pupil injuries will, in all probability, never be eliminated entirely, but when appropiate care is exercised, teacher negligence can be.

Review Questions

1. What rights of redress are maintained by the pupil and the parents for injuries incurred in connection with any school activity?
2. What basic factors govern the corporate liability of school districts and school boards?
3. What are the four primary elements on which an action for negligence can be sustained?
4. What is usually accepted as the first test in determining whether or not there has been negligence on the part of the teacher? Of what does it consist?
5. Who normally has the responsibility of determining whether or not there has been an act of negligence in a liability suit resulting from a school-related pupil injury?
6. What are some of the common conditions under which a teacher is likely to be considered negligent should a pupil injury occur? What is generally the most significant?
7. What is meant by "legal cause?" By *res ipsa loquitur?*
8. What bearing might the actions of a third person have on the determination of negligence and the assessment of damages?

9. How do the responsibilities of a shop teacher for student control compare with those of a lecture/discussion classroom teacher? With those of a chemistry teacher? With those of a physical education teacher?
10. Under what circumstances can assumption of risk and contributory negligence be considered as a defense for a teacher?
11. How do the principles of contributory negligence and comparative negligence differ in application? In what ways are they similar?
12. Describe the social, moral, and economic implications of comparative negligence.
13. What are some of the basic arguments against universal adoption of the principle of comparative negligence?
14. What is understood by the term "proximate cause?" How does it apply to liability suits resulting from school-related pupil injuries?
15. How does the application of the principles of assumption of risk and contributory negligence vary when applied to the rights of minors?
16. What are the discernible trends in the field of law affecting teacher liability?

CHAPTER 3

The Nature and Extent of Shop-Teacher Liability

PUPILS in the public schools of most states are required by law to attend school between the ages of six and sixteen. They are obligated to abide by the rules and regulations of a given school and are expected to engage in certain learning activities. Expanding educational programs of a technical nature in which pupils are permitted or required to operate industrial-type machinery, handle hot liquids or solids, and experiment with caustic or explosive chemicals are bound to increase the hazards to the pupils and to increase the liability of those who may be held responsible for them. Since the pupils are required to attend school, it stands to reason that they do not voluntarily subject themselves to hazards.

Statistics compiled by the National Safety Council reveal that approximately 9 percent of reported school accidents, or about one out of every 11, will take place in the school shop. Shop teachers should be aware of these facts, not only for the physical well-being of the pupils, but also because of the grave consequences that may stem either directly or indirectly from an accident. The effects of the primary principles of liability on shop teachers and the bearing that this relationship has on the conditions under which they work is of prime consideration. In addition, teachers of shop subjects should be cognizant of the circumstances under which liability suits have been filed and the legal framework which governs a teacher's responsibility.

The obligations involved in protecting pupils from accidental injury have assumed major significance. The importance and seriousness of the problem is exemplified in *Hess* v. *School District of the City of Harrisburg*(*1*). The plaintiff's son lost his life after being struck by a piece of wood in the school shop. The piece of wood was being turned in a lathe by the pupil when it disintegrated, causing his death.

This case is unusual because the facts brought out during the trial revealed that although the piece of wood was being turned by the pupil during regularly scheduled and supervised class time, it was intended for use in a stool being constructed for a teacher other than the shop teacher. The court, in ruling in favor of the school district, invoked the principle of governmental immunity.

Perhaps one of the more bizarre school shop accidents in recent years resulted in the death of a junior high student. Evidence submitted verified that the student, while searching for a piece of wood during a regular class session, entered the materials storeroom without authorization. It was determined that approximately 12 sheets of plywood, weighing from 40 to 60 pounds each, fell, pinning the student against the wall and causing strangulation. The deceased student's parents brought suit against the school district charging negligence on the part of the teacher and the school district(*2*).

The court, in ruling in favor of the plaintiffs, found the teacher and the school district guilty of negligence in the manner in which the sheets of plywood were stored. This decision was rendered in spite of the fact that the student had violated an established rule by entering the storeroom alone and without the teacher's permission. Further investigation revealed that the storeroom was usually kept locked.

Law and the Public School

To understand more adequately the position teachers occupy in the public schools with regard to the law, it is important to realize the function of the state in relation to the public school system. The distinction between the state and local autonomy is better understood when it is realized that while, from an administrative standpoint, the regulation of public school pupils is a local problem, legally it is a state problem. Public education is a function of the state, while the actual business of educating the children rests largely with the local district. A public school is an educational institution, as well as an agency of the government.

(*1*) *Hess* v. *School District of City of Harrisburg,* 69 Dauph. 77. Pennsylvania 1956.

(*2*) *Swartley* v. *Seattle School District #1.* 421 P.2d 1009. Washington 1966.

School law has been developed by state constitutional and statutory provisions within the framework of the federal constitution. Every state constitution makes some mention of public education, and directs the state legislature to establish and maintain a system of free public schools. State statutes enacted by state legislatures are the most prolific source of school law. Case law, based on judicial opinions, provides another source. Court decisions are primarily interpretations of constitutional and statutory law and the applications of common-law principles. It is an accepted doctrine that a decision establishing a legal principle stands as a precedent until overruled.

Common Law

Common law is based on legal principles derived from usage and custom, or from court decisions affirming such usages and customs. This distinguishes it from law created by enactments of the legislature. The common law is a result of reasonable action befitting a certain situation and based on the precedent of previous decisions. The principles of common law are brought to bear on situations or circumstances which have not been affected by legislation.

When a practice is challenged by an aggrieved party and there is no statute on the subject, the court may have to resort to common-law principles to decide whether or not the practice is objectionable. The court must determine its findings on the basis of these general principles handed down traditionally over the years.

Common-law tradition is not changed by a statutory law unless it is clearly designed to do so. Statutes have been enacted with the apparent intent of changing the common law, only to have them interpreted by the courts as merely a reiteration of the common-law principle because the language was not sufficiently clear as to intent. This emphasizes the basic fact that any legislation designed to abrogate the common law is strictly construed by the courts.

Statutory Law

Statutory law consists of the statutes enacted by the legislature of any sovereign state. In almost every case involving liability for personal injury resulting from an employee's negligent act, the courts have ruled out the liability of the school district unless there is a specific statute to the contrary.

Judicial interpretation has made it clear that nothing short of an express statute will allow a school district to be subject to payment for damages arising out of acts or omissions of the board while acting in its governmental capacity. Statutes enacted by the legislatures of a few states have made it possible for injured persons to recover damages for injuries. Most prominent among these are statutes making the subdivision liable in tort or enabling the school district to purchase liability insurance. Courts have held generally, however, that a school district does not waive its immunity to tort by the purchase of liability insurance.

Several states have chosen other alternatives in modifying their approach to statutory law relating to public schools. Indiana has limited the extent of liability of any governmental entity. This action came as a result of a breakdown of sovereign immunity and a resultant mushrooming number of liability suits. South Carolina now provides for liability insurance protecting school personnel against liability arising in the course of their employment. Similarly, Utah protects employees and officers of public entities from personal liability arising from acts committed during the performance of their duties and within the scope of their employment. In more recent developments, several states have consented to be sued in tort by passing State Tort Claims Statutes often modeled after the Federal Tort Claims Act. These acts are narrowly construed and prohibit suit unless they clearly give the injured party authority to sue. In North Carolina, the North Carolina Industrial Commission is assigned the responsibility of hearing and passing upon tort claims against departments, institutions, and agencies of the state. If the negligence of the agency involved is found to be the proximate cause of the injury, the Commission determines the amount of damages and directs payments of them by the agency concerned.

School Law

State departments of education periodically publish a compilation of state laws relating to education. These publications are available for use by educators and are usually called school laws. The school or the school district can, therefore, use these school laws as a framework within which they can operate.

There are states which clearly define in their school laws the accepted policy in regard to pupil injuries and the liability of teachers. In other states, the school laws deal more directly with the school districts and do not specifically mention or make implications concerning the individual teacher in this regard.

An example of laws dealing more directly with the school district are the school laws of Virginia(3). The Virginia law states that, "A school

(3) *Virginia School Laws,* Vol. XXXIII, October 1950, No. 5, p. 36.

board is not, in the absence of a statute imposing it, subject to liability for injuries to pupils of public schools suffered in connection with their attendance thereat. And the board is not liable for injuries occurring to individuals, other than pupils, while attending school functions." Furthermore, the school laws of Virginia specifically state that, "A school board is not liable for injuries to pupils received while working in an industrial-arts shop or science laboratory, or while playing on the grounds during recess."

The school laws of New York(*4*), however, indicate an approach more in favor of the individual teacher in respect to liability. In this state, the laws require each board of education to protect all teachers from financial loss arising out of a claim or judgment resulting from an accidental injury to a pupil by reason of alleged negligence, provided that the teacher was acting in the discharge of his duties within the scope of his employment at the time of the incident.

The school laws of New Jersey(*5*) also require the board of education in any school district to protect its employees. A restriction is listed in the New Jersey school laws, however, which indicates that the employing board may not be required to provide or defray the fees and expenses of counsel where the suit for damages is instituted on the grounds of alleged use of corporal punishment.

When a state department of education's law publications are arranged in similar sequence and numbered the same as the state code of general laws for that particular state, they are of greater value and easier to use. One disadvantage of state department of education publications of school law is that they tend to become outdated without revision. In view of this fact, it is recommended that state codes of general laws be used whenever available, either instead of, or in connection with, the state department publications.

The principle of common law is in effect in those states which by statute or school law do not assign liability to the school district. In effect, this means that the school districts of these states are not subject to suit for tort. The legal burden then falls on the teacher.

It is probable that in a state which by statute allows the school district to be sued, injured pupils and their parents would be less likely to bring suit against individual teachers. *If the state statutes remain silent on the*

(*4*) *New York State Education Laws,* Title IV, Article 61, Section 3023 (as amended to July 2, 1956).

(*5*) *New Jersey State Laws of 1938 as amended by School Laws 1954-55* 18:5-50.2 and 18:5-50.4.

problem of teacher liability for pupil injuries, it can be stated that teachers are legally responsible for their negligent actions and are therefore subject to liability.

The specific facts in each case are an important factor in any decision that may be rendered. It is unwise for superintendents and school board members to try to be their own attorneys in situations as complicated as school-district liability. Since important differences exist in the legislative enactments and legal interpretations of school laws as they are related to school-district liability, school officials should seek the advice of legal counsel when necessary and be thoroughly acquainted with the statutes and court decisions which relate to school liability.

Plaintiffs have, on occasion, brought actions against several parties when damages are sought, with the apparent hope of gaining some satisfaction from at least one of the parties involved. When multiple defendants are named in a suit, it becomes the responsibility of the court to determine liability, on the basis of the evidence produced, as related to the constitutional and statutory provisions of the state.

The School District

Public education is a governmental function belonging to the state. This means that outside of certain general federal constitutional controls, the state has absolute power in establishing and maintaining public schools. The local school district is a territorial division of the state established by the legislature as an agency of the state government. It has been created for school purposes, having local public education as its only concern. The public schools are operated as governmental subdivisions of the state and are usually separate from other civil units.

The powers of a local school district are limited to those granted to it by statute and those arising out of necessity within the framework of the constitution. Although local school boards have no common-law powers, they are still the administrative body for the school district. No distinction is made between the powers and the duties of a school district and the school board. The school board, although composed of individuals, must be treated as a single unit administratively. The individual members are not subject to suit because of their position. If a liability arises on the part of the school board, it is the board itself, and not its individual members, which is held responsible.

The School District and Common-Law Immunity

The origin for common-law or governmental immunity in the United

States can be traced to a decision rendered in England during the Middle Ages(6) and subsequently to a case decided in Massachusetts in 1812(7). The idea has frequently been expressed as "the King can do no wrong." From this evolved the concept of according a state and its governmental subdivisions the status of sovereign. Accepting the premise of sovereignty, it follows then that the state can do no wrong and cannot be sued without its consent. In line with this reasoning, since a school district is a governmental subdivision and the school board an agency of the state it is immune to tort action.

As early as April 20, 1911, Assistant Attorney General Greenhalge of Massachusetts handed down an opinion which emphasized the fact that the school district, acting as an instrumentality of the Commonwealth within the scope of the duties imposed on it by law, enjoys governmental immunity for liability for torts. The opinion also observed that for accidents resulting from negligence, there would probably be personal liability on the part of the person directly responsible.

In some states the principle of comon-law immunity is adhered to and the courts are consistent in their interpretations. In *Krutili* v. *Board of Education of Butler District*(8), the board of education was judged not liable by the court due to the common-law ruling of immunity. The plaintiff had charged that the board of education was negligent in maintaining an unguarded planer. In ruling on this case, the court made it plain that the general rule in their county was that a school district, municipal corporation, or school board is not, in the absence of a statute imposing it, subject to liability for injuries to pupils in public schools, suffered in connection with their attendance thereat, since such district, corporation, or board, in maintaining schools, acts as an agent of the state and performs a purely public or governmental duty imposed on it by law for the benefit of the public and for the performance of which it receives no profit or advantage.

Most courts in the United States have, by their decisions, continually accepted the nonliability of school districts. This is based on the grounds that the school district is a quasi-corporation with limited powers, or because there is no fund to meet such damages, or on the point of law that the legal relation of master and servant does not exist between the district and its employees.

---

(6) *Russell* v. *The Men of Devon,* 100 Eng. Rep. 359 2 T.R. 667 (England 1788).

(7) *Mower* v. *Leicester,* 9 Mass. 247. Massachusetts 1812.

(8) *Krutili* v. *Board of Education of Butler District,* 129 S.E. 486. West Virginia 1925.

Governmental immunity applies equally to state universities and state colleges as well as to public elementary and secondary schools. This is evidenced in *Todd* v. *Curators of the University of Missouri*(9) and in a 1960 opinion by Kansas Attorney General John Anderson. Anderson stated that the state board of regents is an arm of state government and immune to being sued except as expressly authorized by statute.

Seemingly valid reasons have been given for the continuance of the common-law principle of immunity as applied to school districts. In addition to the fact that school districts are in reality agents of the state in performing public or governmental functions, it has also been emphasized that school funds are trust funds set aside for the sole purpose of maintaining schools and cannot be diverted from the use imposed on them. Special legislation is required to authorize payment of damages from school funds and it has been felt by many that the quality of education programs might suffer if funds were diverted for this purpose. Budgets would pose extreme problems because of the uncertain element of damages. Another legitimate reason for the continuance of governmental immunity stems from the fear of an unusual number of lawsuits which could serve to hamper effective school administration.

The principle of common-law immunity is based on the assumption that the individual's interest in being reimbursed for injuries must yield to the greater interest of the general public. In keeping with this assumption, there are those courts which believe that the most logical solution to the problem is the application of the principle of *laissez faire* (noninterference). This would relieve the school district of any liability for negligence by permitting common-law immunity to remain in effect.

The principle of governmental immunity of the school district has been upheld even though it was proven in court that the machine on which the injury took place was improperly guarded. The case of *Conrad* v. *Board of Education of Ridgeville Township*(10) is an example where no recovery was allowed, although negligence of the defendant board was conceded. Injury to the plaintiff occurred while he was operating an improperly guarded power saw in the school shop. The court in ruling on this case stated:

> In the absence of a statute specifically creating a civil liability, a board of education is not liable in damages to a pupil who is taking

---

(9) *Todd* v. *Curators of the University of Missouri,* 147 S.W.2d 1063. Missouri 1941.

(10) *Conrad* v. *Board of Education of Ridgeville Township,* 163 N.E. 567. Ohio 1928.

> a manual training course in its mechanical department, and who suffers injury as a result of the board's failure to protect, as required by law, the machinery used by said pupil.

Common-law immunity of the school district was again sustained in *Niedfelt* v. *Joint School District No. 1 of City of Viroqua*(*11*). The plaintiff brought action after suffering severe injuries to his left hand and arm while he was operating an unguarded power table saw. The court invoked the common-law principle in ruling for the defendant school district and denied any claim for damages.

Courts on occasion have disallowed the protective umbrella of governmental immunity as it pertains to school districts. Such was the case in *Scott County School District #1* v. *Asher*(*12*). Action was brought on behalf of a 16-year-old high-school student against the school district. The plaintiff sought to recover damages for a severe hand injury sustained while operating a power bench saw in a shop class. Negligence was charged, alleging that the school had permitted the saw to be installed and maintained improperly. The circuit court entered judgment in favor of the student and the school district appealed. However, in spite of a concern for proximate cause, the Court of Appeals upheld the lower court decision and ruled that the defense of govenmental immunity was not available to the school district. The court awarded the injured student $95,000 in damages. The damages were based on the loss of potential earnings, deformity, and disfigurement.

Related aspects of the common law of governmental immunity affect the legal regulations governing a school district. Paramount among these is the fact that under this doctrine, the school district has no legal authority to purchase insurance, unless specifically authorized to do so by statute. The reasoning behind this is that a school district cannot spend money to insure itself against a liability to which it is not subject.

Significant doubt is now being raised with regard to the doctrine of nonliability of school districts for torts. Since it is the American tradition to disregard or to change doctrines which have become obsolete, it is felt that progress will be made to modify the common-law immunity of school districts to more nearly fit the times.

Modifications of Common-Law Immunity

A review of court cases and opinions handed down by the courts reveals

---

(*11*) *Niedfelt* v. *Joint School District No. 1 of City of Viroqua*, 127 N.W.2d 618. Wisconsin 1962.

(*12*) *Scott County School District #1* v. *Asher*, 312 N.E.2d 131. Indiana 1974.

that all are not in sympathy with the common-law principle of nonliability as applied to school districts. There are those who feel that a school district should not maintain the right to hide behind this principle when it is negligent in its duties. As a result of *Bragg* v. *Board of Public Instruction of Duval County*(13), Judge Terrell of the Florida Supreme Court, gave the following opinion:

> Some time in the future, legislatures, whose duty it is to provide such legislation, will see fit to spread the damages occasioned by shop accidents and society will be required to help bear the burden of such unfortunate incidents.

Judge Terrell's opinion was to prove prophetic. The doctrine of governmental immunity has since been abrogated in the State of Florida.

Some authors in the field of school law believe that governmental immunity, as applied to school districts, is old, obsolete, and unjust. Dissenting judges have referred to governmental immunity as an anachronism. It has been frequently stated that since education has become big business, the immunity rule has been lost in antiquity and should be abrogated in its entirety. Education programs which subject pupils to potential hazards such as the use of power machinery, chemicals in the laboratory, and possible injuries from athletic contests should be expected to compensate for such injuries as a legitimate cost of education.

Courts, which have upheld the principle of governmental immunity, have emphasized through their decisions that no school district can accept liability voluntarily and waive its immunity. The reason for this is quite clear when it is realized that a school district is a subordinate unit without the power to make itself liable and that the waiving of governmental immunity usually requires state legislation.

Although, in general, the rule of governmental immunity remains throughout the country, some states have seen fit to adjust the law to their own situations, thereby becoming exceptions to the theory of sovereignty. These states include California, in which the school district accepts liability for nearly all accidents; New York, Connecticut, and New Jersey, where a school district will reimburse a teacher for any judgment he might be required to pay; Washington, which will allow certain general liability for specific situations (although not for school-shop accidents); and Iowa. Action of the Iowa Legislature eliminated the immunity of school districts and other units of local government to tort

---

(13) *Bragg* v. *Board of Public Instruction of Duval County,* 36 S.2d 222. Florida 1948.

liability in the summer of 1967. The same legislation made Iowa a "save-harmless" state effective January 1, 1968, in addition to authorizing local governing bodies to purchase liability insurance.

The Illinois Supreme Court took exception to the nonliability principle when it ruled on the case of *Molitor* v. *Kaneland Community Unit School District*(*14*). In a most significant development, the court overthrew and negated the doctrine of governmental immunity as applied to school districts in action for damages for tort. In doing so, the court completely changed the legal doctrine relating to Illinois schools and ruled that school districts are to be held liable in tort for the negligence of their employees, thereby setting aside all prior decisions to the contrary. It was the court's view that abrogation of the immunity rule would encourage the exercise of greater care in the transportation of pupils and tend to decrease the frequency of school-bus accidents. The court acted on the supposition that the principle of common-law immunity as applied to school districts is unjust, unsupported by any valid reason, and has no rightful place in modern-day public education. This is a modern development, and it is likely that this decision will motivate or encourage the high courts of other states to take similar action.

As a direct result of the decision of the Illinois Supreme Court in *Molitor* v. *Kaneland Unit School District*, the Illinois General Assembly passed legislation, which became effective July 22, 1959, limiting recovery on each cause of action for negligence brought against school districts or nonprofit schools to $10,000. This limitation has been challenged without success in several court actions involving school districts.

Although the full impact of this case is yet to be felt, five additional states followed the precedent set by Illinois and abrogated the principle of common-law immunity by Supreme Court decision. These states include Wisconsin(*15*), Arizona(*16*), Nebraska(*17*), New Jersey(*18*), and Colorado(*19*). None of these actions grew out of a school-shop injury and

---

(*14*) *Molitor* v. *Kaneland Community Unit School District*, 155 N.E.2d 841. Illinois 1959.

(*15*) *Holtz* v. *City of Milwaukee*, 155 N.W.2d 618. Wisconsin 1962.

(*16*) *Stone* v. *Arizona State Highway Commission*, 381 P.2d 107. Arizona 1963.

(*17*) *Johnson* v. *Municipal University of Omaha*, 169 N.W.2d 287. Nebraska 1969.

(*18*) *Willis* v. *Department of Conservation and Economic Development*, 264 A.2d 34. New Jersey 1970.

(*19*) *Flournoy* v. *School District No. 1 in the City and County of Denver*, 482 P.2d 966. Colorado 1971.

only two actually involved schools. Nevertheless, school districts are directly affected since they are classified as governmental subdivisions and all such state divisions fall under the general application of these decisions. The defendant in the Nebraska case was the Municipal University of Omaha while the defendant named in the Colorado litigation was School District No. 1 in the City and County of Denver. The defendant in the Wisconsin case was the City of Milwaukee; in Arizona, the State Highway Commission; and in New Jersey, the Department of Conservation and Economic Development. Prior to this, New Jersey had enacted common-law immunity into statutory form*(20)*.

The Minnesota Supreme Court overruled governmental immunity as a defense in actions against all government entities in *Spanel* v. *Moundsview School District(21)*, but the 1963 Legislature subsequently restored the immunity rule as a defense in actions against school districts. However, the Legislature provided that when a school district procures liability insurance it becomes subject to the statutory provisions to the extent of the coverage obtained. Although the principle of governmental immunity was set aside earlier by Supreme Court decision in Missouri*(22)* and Michigan*(23)*, it has now been ruled that the abrogation does apply to school districts in these states.

High courts in other states have continued the erosion and abrogation of the common-law doctrine as it applies to public education. The number of states which have chosen to judicially abrogate the doctrine of governmental immunity has now grown to 19, plus the District of Columbia. A prime example is Pennsylvania which had retained common-law immunity until the 1973 decision handed down in *Ayala* vs. *Philadelphia Board of Education(24)*. The issue in this case was governmental immunity, not the injuries sustained. The action was brought against the Board of Education for injuries sustained by a student who caught his arm in a shredding machine in an upholstery class. The Court of Common Pleas rendered judgment for the defendant school district in deference to the principle of immunity. The plaintiffs appealed. The Supreme Court reversed the

---

(20) Public Laws of New Jersey, 1933, Ch. 460, p. 1550 (rev. stat. 18:5-30, 4:0-2).

(21) Spanel v. *Moundsview School District No. 621,* 118 N.W.2d 795. Minnesota 1962.

(22) Prewitt v. *Parkway School District,* 557 S.W.2d 232. Missouri 1977.

(23) Pittman v. *City of Taylor,* 247 N.W.2d 512. Michigan 1977.

(24) Ayala v. *Philadelphia Board of Public Education,* 305 A.2d 877. Pennsylvania 1973.

decision of the lower court and remanded the case for further action, holding that the doctrine of governmental immunity is abolished as applied to the determination in this case. In taking this action, the court ruled that the judiciously imposed doctrine of governmental immunity could be judiciously terminated.

School administrators and teachers should be aware that a change is taking place and be alert for developments which are expected to materialize. Pressure may be applied to state legislatures encouraging the enactment of laws specifically making the school districts liable, or actually rendering them immune by statutory law. Legislation may also be requested to limit liability to the extent of insurance held by the school district, or legislation may be requested that the amount of liability be limited in any one case.

Legal Status of the Teacher

The position of a public school teacher is created by the legislature with the powers and duties fixed to a large extent by law. It has been established that a teacher is not a public officer, is not immune from liability because employed by a governmental agency, and can be held personally liable for acts of negligence while performing his duties as a teacher. A teacher is also governed by the common-law obligation that every person must so act, or use that which he controls, so as not to injure another. What the law requires of the teacher is that he exercise that care and prudence any reasonably prudent person would have exercised in the same or similar situation. The position a teacher maintains in regard to the pupils under his care may be the deciding factor in establishing whether or not he is to be held liable in the event of a pupil injury.

The standard of care owed by teachers to pupils under their guidance and supervision is a question frequently placed before the courts and often is the crux of tort liability resulting from school-related student injuries. The Vermont Supreme Court said it well when it stated, "A teacher owes his pupils a degree of supervision, and if there is a failure to exercise reasonable care in carrying out this duty, either in the commission or omission of an act which results in injury, the teacher is liable to the pupil."

An opinion handed down by Harold R. Fatzer, Attorney General, state of Kansas, on August 11, 1953, pointed out that there is some difference of opinion among courts as to the liability of school teachers for injuries to pupils. However, he observed that, in the absence of a decision by the supreme court of the state, it is impossible to state categorically whether or not teachers would be liable for injuries to pupils, although it appears that there is a good chance of liability for acts of misfeasance in the performance of ministerial duties.

Although many characteristics of the work suggest that the position a public school teacher occupies is a public office, the courts have been almost unanimous in classifying teachers as employees rather than officers. This distinction is important because if teachers were school officers, their status would be materially affected by the body of law dealing with public officers in general.

Classroom teachers are more closely involved in pupil activities than any other members of the school staff and are more often named as defendants in cases alleging negligence. Since each individual is held responsible for his own negligence, a teacher who is found negligent can be held legally responsible and subject to payment of damages. It must be clearly understood that before a teacher can be held liable, it must be proved that the negligence of the teacher was the proximate cause of the incurred injury.

In Loco Parentis

The legal aspects of a teacher's relationship with pupils is contained in the phrase, *in loco parentis*. This means "In place of the parent." *In loco parentis* is an ancient legal doctrine under which the teachers become parents pro tem; that is, they have some of the rights and duties of the parent. In the faithful discharge of such duties, the teacher is bound to use reasonable care, tested in the light of the existing relationship.

The principle of *in loco parentis* is presumed to have evolved when the earliest teachers were employed to spare parents some of the work entailed in raising children. As the teachers took over some of the parental responsibilites, they acquired privileges and duties in some degree identical to those of the parents. This principle has undergone a period of evolution and the school now derives its authority from the whole body of organized society. The extent of control a teacher is allowed to exert is limited to situations which are related to the purposes of education and training of the pupils.

The feelings of the courts regarding the principle of *in loco parentis* are illustrated in *Brooks* v. *Jacobs*(25). Direct action was brought against a high school shop teacher for injuries sustained by a pupil when he fell from a staging which had been erected around a vocational-training building being constructed with pupil assistance. The pupil, who was

---

(25) *Brooks* v. *Jacobs*, 31 A.2d 414. Maine 1943.

working under the defendant's instruction, was injured when the staging gave way. The pupil charged the teacher with negligence in allowing a defective staging to be used. The court, in finding for the plaintiff, ruled that the teacher was negligent in his relationship to the plaintiff and that he did not act as a reasonable and prudent parent would have acted under similar or the same circumstances.

In ruling on this case, Judge Hudson of the Maine Supreme Court stated:

> An instructor, accepting responsibility of due care toward persons under his direction and control, must exercise such care, not only as to what he himself actually does on observance of such duty, but as to what he fails to do which he should have done in the exercise of due care.

The teacher was declared negligent in his duty in not inspecting the scaffolding before allowing the pupil to work on it. From this it can be seen that even though teachers are said to stand *in loco parentis* with regard to the pupils under their care, they are still liable for injuries which may involve damages. This, in effect, establishes the legal duty of teachers to care for school pupils. Every teacher, administrator, and board member works as a parent pro tem under this doctrine.

The Teacher and Common-Law Immunity

Although school districts are granted exemption from the normal liability associated with school-related pupil injuries, such immunity does not apply to teachers as individuals. Teachers do not gain the advantage of immunity because they are public employees. In fact, they may be held even more accountable than the ordinary layman because pupils are entrusted to their care, and teachers accept the duty of preventing pupil injuries insofar as possible. There have been court cases resulting from pupil injuries brought jointly against the teacher and the school district in which the school district was declared immune and the teacher held liable (*26*).

Much of the problem of assessment of liability for pupil injuries centers around the sovereign immunity of school districts and the teacher's personal liability, which largely depends on the common-law principles of negligence. When dealing with pupils, the law requires the teacher to exercise that care and prudence that any reasonable person would have exercised in the same or a similar circumstance.

(*26*) *Woodman* v. *Hemet Union High School District,* 29 P.2d 257. California 1934.

The court protected the school district under the common-law rule in *Crabbe* v. *County School Board of Northumberland County*(27), but denied the same protection to the teacher. Charges were brought when the plaintiff suffered a permanent hand injury while operating a power table saw in the wood laboratory. The plaintiff alleged that not only was the saw defective and improperly equipped, but that these facts were known to the teacher. The court, in denying a damage claim against the school district, indicated that the plaintiff had good cause for action against the teacher in that the teacher had failed to properly instruct on the use of the saw. The case was remanded for a new trial.

The question of whether or not the doctrine of sovereign immunity extends to the teacher was raised in *Duncan* v. *Koustenis*(28). The student, who had parts of two fingers severed in an industrial arts class, claimed the teacher was negligent in improperly attaching a guard on an automatic planer. The trial court dismissed the charges against the teacher and the student appealed.

The Maryland Court of Appeals ruled that governmental immunity does extend to nonmalicious acts of *public officials* acting in a discretionary capacity, but not to *public employees.* The Court further ruled that teachers are public employees and do not qualify as public officials. The Court held that public officials hold positions clearly distinguishable from that of a teacher. In applying the test of who is a public official, the court found a teacher would not qualify for the following reasons: A teacher is not required to take an official oath of office, receives no commission, gives no bond, is not commonly thought of as an officer, and does not exercise sovereign powers of government. The court accordingly held that teachers are not public officials, but are professional contract employees and that the doctrine of sovereign immunity does not apply to them. The judgment of the trial court was reversed and the case remanded for further proceedings.

The shop teacher is directly affected by the nonliability of school districts. He is a prime target for litigation because each individual is liable for his own torts. Since the possibility of a claim of negligent action against a shop teacher is considerable, due to the kinds of activities in which pupils engage in shop classes, it is imperative that shop teachers furnish adequate pupil supervision to escape the charge of negligence.

---

(27) *Crabbe* v. *County School Board of Northumberland County,* 164 S.E.2d 639. Virginia 1968.

(28) *Duncan* v. *Koustenis,* 271 A.2d 547. Maryland 1970.

School-Shop Accidents

The possibility of accidents in industrial education classes is considerable because of the nature of the activities which are a normal part of the learning process. When an accident in a school shop causes serious injury or involves financial consideration, a legal action may result. Various reasons have been used to establish liability on the teacher's part for injured pupils, but research indicates that negligence is the most common.

In addition to the cases taken to court, there are many school-shop accidents which are never litigated for one reason or another. Many of these are of interest, however, because of the circumstances surrounding the accidents and the related effects on the school program.

Litigated Shop Accidents

Legal actions carried to the appellate or highest court of any state for disposition become cases of printed record and are recorded in the National Reporter System. These are not the sum total of all cases, as there are many others which have been resolved in the lower courts or are settled before they are actually brought to trial.

Court cases usually result when a person feels he has been aggrieved and, in particular, where financial interests are involved. The decisions of the courts become useful as sources of information and, although they do not have the effect of binding laws and are not always in agreement, they do indicate trends. They also serve as criteria in cases where doubt exists and may become guides to action.

A review of the National Reporter System indicates that one of the first cases of record resulting from a school-shop accident occurred in 1920*(29)*. The plaintiff, who was injured on a circular saw in the industrial education department of the school, charged that the school district was negligent in the care and operation of the machine. The court, in ruling for the school district, invoked the principle of governmental immunity.

In relation to this case, it is interesting to note that the governmental immunity of school districts was abrogated in the State of Washington in 1869. However, in 1917 this law was modified by an act which barred actions against school districts for noncontractual acts or omissions of officers relating to park, playground, or manual-training equipment. This act purported to relieve school districts and their officers from liability for injuries resulting from the use of the industrial education equipment of schools in the state of Washington.

---

(29) *Swanson* v. *School District No. 15 Pierce County,* 187 P. 386. Washington 1920.

In 1961, the Washington Supreme Court upheld the 1917 statute prohibiting suits against Washington school districts for accidents relating to industrial education equipment(*30*). The court, in declaring the school district immune from any liability for any negligence, reiterated that the school district's operation of the school constituted an exercise of a governmental function. It was also ruled that although a 1953 statute repealed certain laws, it did not expressly, nor by implication, repeal the 1917 statute dealing with industrial education equipment.

Action was instigated when Teddy Lee Babcock, a minor, suffered permanent injuries to his left hand while operating a table saw in a schoolshop. This action was brought to recover damages for injuries sustained due to alleged acts of negligence on the part of the school district.

In another action early in the history of litigation of school-shop accidents, the power saw was also the machine involved(*31*). The decision in favor of the school district was based on the principle of common-law immunity. In summarizing the facts of this case, the court stated that instruction in "manual training" involved the valid use of mechanical devices.

Certain tools and machines in the school shop appear to have a higher accident rate and injury factor than others. The power table or bench saw is a case in point and has figured in a number of accidental injuries leading to litigation. In most cases, the injuries are confined to the fingers and hands, but on occasion extend to other parts of the body. Circumstances vary as to the cause of accidents, but usually relate to conditions of the machine itself, absence of safety features, or lack of insistence that safety devices be used. Charges of negligence then ensue and are brought against the teacher and/or the school district.

An Indiana case featured an action against a school district and the manufacturer of a power table saw when a student lost four fingers as a result of an accident(*32*). Facts of the case verify that the student was injured while operating a 10-inch power table saw in an unsupervised industrial arts classroom. The 14-year-old 9th grade student and a classmate had gone to the shop during a study period to cut pieces of wood which the teacher intended to use later in the day for another class. The teacher was teaching a drafting class in an adjacent room that was separated

---

(*30*) *Babcock* v. *School District No. 17 of Clallam County*, 358 P.2d 547. Washington 1961.

(*31*) *Sullivan* v. *School District No. 1 of City of Tomah*, 191 N.W. 1020. Wisconsin 1923.

(*32*) *South Ripley Community School Corporation* v. *Peters and Powermatic-Houdaille*, 396 N.E.2d 144. Indiana 1979.

from the wood shop by a glass partition. While cutting wooden blocks, the blade stalled in a piece of wood and the student was injured in attempting to dislodge the wood from the blade without turning off the power. Although the saw was equipped with guards, one was ineffective because it was broken. The jury, in ruling on this case, found in favor of the saw manufacturer but against the school district. Judgment was entered against the school district in favor of the plaintiff for $75,000 and in favor of the parents for an additional $25,000.

On occasion, university and college students are involved in litigation resulting from injuries sustained while using power equipment in shops and laboratories. In *Segal* v. *State of New York and State University of New York College at Purchase*(33), an action was brought against the state for injuries sustained by a university student who suffered severe lacerations to the left hand and loss of the left index finger while operating a power table saw. The negligence claim was based on a failure to supervise, promulgate, and enforce rules and regulations. It was further alleged that the saw itself was inherently dangerous and hazardous.

The court, in ruling in favor of the state, declared that the state was not derelict in its duty of supervision. Facts of the case confirmed that the student was injured by a power saw which she was not required to use and which she had not been given permission to use. Evidence showed that an adequate degree of supervision had been provided and the student was declared guilty of contributory negligence. It was substantiated in court that students were not authorized to use the power saw but were instructed to rely on paid student assistants for tasks of this nature.

Another case involving injuries resulting from the use of a power table saw was decided in favor of the Board of Education when the student was declared contributorily negligent on his own injuries(34). The 16-year-old plaintiff had lost the first joint of his right index finger in the school-shop accident involving a power saw. The trial court was supported by the Appellate Division which permitted the jury to pass upon the knowledge, experience, and conduct of the student. The decision was affirmed without cause.

Sewell v. *London*(35) involved a vocational building trades class and a portable power saw. A 16-year-old student in the class was severely in-

---

(33) *Segal* v. *State of New York and State University of New York at Purchase,* 359 N.Y.S.2d 498. New York 1974.

(34) *Ressel* v. *Board of Education of the Great Amsterdam School District,* 395 N.Y.S.2d 263. New York 1977.

(35) *Sewell* v. *London,* 371 S.W.2d 426. Texas 1963.

jured while ripping 1 × 6s with the portable power saw as assigned by the teacher. The injury occurred when the saw bounded out of the board being cut, swung upwards as high as the student's head, and came down on his right hand, cutting his fingers and causing him to release the saw. The saw subsequently fell on the student's left leg, gashing his thigh and then falling to the ground. The student testified that because of a defective switch, the saw remained running until it hit the ground. The student brought litigation against the teacher claiming negligence for allowing defective equipment to be used in the class. The District Court entered a summary judgment denying the plaintiff a recovery and the plaintiff appealed. The Court of Civil Appeals held that there were sufficient doubts regarding the condition of the portable power saw and the lack of a clearly defined proximate cause to revise the lower court decision and remand for further action.

In reviewing the history of cases of record growing out of school-shop accidents, it is apparent that the incident rate has increased during the past decade. It is difficult to clearly assess the reasons, but it has been observed that students and parents have been more active particpants in litigation. More shop-related accidents ended in court action from 1971-1980 than in any other period in the history of school-shop liability. The wood shop has taken the lead in this category with the metals laboratory a fairly close second. It should be pointed out, however, that with the exception of drafting, more junior high and high school students enroll in wood shop and metal shop classes than any other vocational-technical-industrial activity. Power machines were involved in more than 60 percent of the accidents resulting in court cases.

A direct action charging negligence was brought against a shop teacher as a result of an accident which did not involve power machines(*36*). The injured pupil sustained serious burns when an allegedly uncorked bottle of acid spilled on him in an unsupervised oil room (finishing room). The facts of this case were judged on the common law of negligence and not on any statutory law. The lower court found the shop teacher (defendant) 55 percent negligent and the pupil (plaintiff) 45 percent negligent. This, in effect, was a verdict for the pupil in view of the comparative negligence laws which are in effect in Wisconsin. A verdict of 50 percent negligence for each constituent would have nullified the case.

The Milwaukee County Circuit Court entered a judgment notwithstanding the verdict and dismissed the complaint. The plaintiff thereupon appealed and the case was referred to the Supreme Court. The Su-

(*36*) *Grosso* v. *Witteman,* 62 N.W.2d 386. Wisconsin 1954.

preme Court affirmed the decision of the Circuit Court and held that the plaintiff did not prove that the teacher had not corked the acid bottle in question and furthermore did not prove negligence on the part of the teacher. The teacher was thereby absolved of any liability or damages.

Wisconsin's comparative negligence law was also invoked in *Severson* v. *City of Beloit*(37). This litigation involved an adult vocational student who was enrolled in a night class for the purpose of upgrading his skills as a grinder. The injury occurred shortly after the plaintiff turned a switch activating the multiple-speed grinder. The grinding wheel fragmented, causing serious injury to the student. The court found the adult vocational student 25 percent negligent and the city and school district 75 percent negligent. The student was awarded $15,000 of a $20,000 damage claim. The court based its findings on allegations of inadequate advanced instruction, inadequate teacher supervision, failure on the part of the teacher to enforce safety regulations, and a total lack of warning. In addition, it was found that the grinder was improperly guarded.

Common-law immunity was the principle of law involved in deciding the outcome of one case involving a printing press(38), and the safety regulations of a state division of industrial safety respecting the guarding of machines in another(39). In the first instance, the plaintiff's right arm and hand were lacerated and bruised and his fingers severed while operating a printing press. Although the plaintiff suffered injuries while operating the press in the performance of a required part of the high-school curriculum, the county board of public instruction was held immune by virtue of the principle of common-law immunity.

In the second case, also involving a printing press, the plaintiff's hand was caught and injured in the press. It was charged by the plaintiff that the school district was negligent in failing to provide a proper guard on the printing press. The Superior Court of Los Angeles County entered judgment for the defendant and the plaintiff appealed. In reversing the decision of the Superior Court of Los Angeles County, the District Court of Appeal held that safety regulations of the state division of industrial safety respecting the guarding of machines were applicable to school districts. The school district was, therefore, held negligent because of nonconformance to this code and liable for the injuries sustained by the

(37) *Severson* v. *City of Beloit*, 167 N.W.2d 258. Wisconsin 1969.

(38) *Bragg* v. *Board of Public Instruction of Duval County*, 36 S.2d 222. Florida 1948.

(39) *Lehman* v. *Los Angeles City Board of Education*, 316 P.2d 55. California 1957.

plaintiff.

Seven cases of record since World War II involved the loss of an eye by the plaintiff. In three of the cases, the courts found for the plaintiff, and in four ruled for the defendant board of education.

The common-law principle of governmental immunity was affirmed in *Campbell* v. *Board of Education*(40). A claim for damages was brought following an accident in the metals laboratory in which a metal particle from a machine entered the eye of the plaintiff, causing a permanent eye injury.

In another case in which the court found in favor of the board of education(41), the plaintiff suffered permanent injury to his left eye as a result of being struck by a drawing pencil thrown in a mechanical drawing class. The teacher was absent from the classroom at the time of the injury. Even though it was substantiated in court that the teacher was out of the room when the pencil was thrown and the pupil injured, the court ruled for the defendant and said:

> It does not follow that absence from the classroom was the producing cause of the injury, which was due, as we see it, to the tossed pencil. Whether it was done mischievously and heedlessly or wantonly and willfully, or with the serious purpose of returning the pencil to its owner, it was the act of an intervening third party which under the circumstances could hardly have been anticipated in the reasonable exercise of the teacher's legal duty toward the plaintiff. Under common-law standards, a teacher may be charged only with reasonable care.

A ruling similar to that handed down in the Ohman case was rendered in *Butler* v. *District of Columbia*(42). The plaintiff suffered permanent damage when hit in the eye by a sharp object, presumably a piece of type, when he entered the print shop. Although court evidence substantiated the fact that the teacher was not in the classroom at the time of the incident, the court denied the plaintiff's claim of negligence and concluded that the teacher's absence from the classroom did not constitute the proximate cause of the injury. Futher discussion of this case is contained on page 18 in Chapter 2.

The question as to what constitutes absence of the teacher from the

---

(40) *Campbell* v. *Board of Education*, 389 P.2d 464. Utah 1964.

(41) *Ohman* v. *Board of Education of New York*, 90 N.E.2d 474. New York 1949.

(42) *Butler* v. *District of Columbia*, 417 F.2d 1150. District of Columbia 1969.

classroom was a matter of special concern in *Hammond* v. *Scott*(*43*). A student was injured in a woodworking class during a short period the teacher was in the adjacent storeroom assisting other students in storing their class projects. While the teacher was thus involved, a student in the class threw a nail toward a wastebasket and it hit a second student in the eye. This student subsequently lost sight in the eye and brought action against the other student and the teacher based on alleged negligence, willfullness, and wantonness. The Common Pleas Court granted summary judgment to the teacher and the plaintiff appealed. The Supreme Court, in affirming the decision of the lower court, held that the teacher's responsibility for the class supervision extended to the project storage room. It was further brought out that the teacher had previously admonished the defendant student for throwing, rather than dropping, objects into the wastebasket. The practice of throwing objects into the wastebasket was not sanctioned by the teacher and the students were well aware that this was a forbidden act in the classroom. The plaintiff's father brought a companion action against the same defendants with a higher court affirming the lower court decision in both instances.

Negligence and lack of foreseeability were the principles of law involved in one of the cases decided for the pupil as plaintiff(*44*). The teacher of a metals class had taken the pupils to the lawn of the school building because of construction noise in the school building proper. The plaintiff suffered permanent eye damage when a knife, which another pupil was playing with, struck a third pupil's drawing board and was deflected into his eye. It was charged that the teacher had failed to supervise the action of the pupil who was playing with the knife, and that this dangerous circumstance would have been foreseen by an ordinarily prudent person.

In a somewhat unusual case of record involving an eye injury(*45*), negligence was charged by the plaintiff, with the defendant school district countering with a charge of contributory negligence on the part of the plaintiff. The charge of contributory negligence was denied and the school district found negligent in the care and maintenance of goggles recommended for use while operating a buffing machine. The pupil suffered the eye injury while polishing silver rings on a set of harness reins,

(*43*) *Hammond* v. *Scott*, 232 S.E.2d 336. South Carolina 1977.

(*44*) *Lilienthal* v. *San Leandro Unified School District*, 298 P. 2d 889. California 1956.

(*45*) *Ross* v. *San Francisco Unified School District*, 260 P.2d 663. California 1953.

pursuant to the shop teacher's orders. The set of reins was the property of the shop teacher. Through the evidence given, it was determined that the goggles had been defective for some time, and that the teacher should have been aware of this condition. The court found the teacher negligent in failing to correct a known dangerous condition, for which this California school district was held liable.

Contributory negligence was denied by the court as a defense for the school districts in two other cases recorded during this period. In the first case(*46*), a pupil had part of his finger cut off on a shearing machine in a metal shop. The accident occurred when another pupil stepped on the foot treadle of the machine from which the plaintiff was attempting to extricate a piece of metal. The teacher was within nine feet of the shearing machine at the time of the accident. The court found for the plaintiff and ruled that, but for the negligence of the teacher, the pupil could not have been injured by a third person's action. Furthermore, it was brought out that the injury was caused by the teacher's concurrent negligence in failing to observe whether or not the machine was being used properly, or was being tampered with by other pupils. Negligence of the city board of education was determined to be the proximate or concurring cause of the injury so as to render the board liable.

In a parallel case brought to trial in North Carolina, a student filed for damages against the community college trustees seeking to recover for injuries he received while operating a metal shearing machine maintained and supplied by the college and under the supervision of the classroom instructor(*47*). The plaintiff sustained the loss of two fingertips which were mashed by the hold-down plunger designed to clamp the metal in place when a foot pedal is depressed. The decision was rendered in favor of the defendant based on the following facts:

a. the plaintiff was adequately warned;
b. the plaintiff did receive proper instruction;
c. the teacher provided adequate demonstrations of the capabilities of the machine;
d. contributory negligence and assumption of risk could be factors;
e. the teacher expressly cautioned the students in the operation of the machine;
f. the plaintiff had operated the shearing machine successfully several

---

(*46*) *DeBennedittis* v. *Board of Education New York City,* 67 N.Y.S.2d 30. New York 1946.

(*47*) *Kiser* v. *Snyder et al.,* 194 S.E.2d 638. North Carolina 1973. And 205 S.E.2d 619. North Carolina 1974.

times prior to the accident;

g. the teacher was not otherwise negligent.

In another case involving contributory negligence*(48)*, the court found in favor of the plaintiff and adjudged the teacher had failed to enforce rules and regulations of safety in the auto shop when he failed to supervise a pupil who was using an acetylene torch near a gas tank. A claim by the teacher and the school district that the accident was unavoidable and that the injured pupils had been contributorily negligent was denied. The accident took place when a pupil, who was not a member of the class in session, was using an acetylene torch to repair his own automobile. Facts brought out in the investigation indicated doubt that the teacher in charge was aware of his presence. Two bona fide members of the class paused to watch the repair work when a spark from the acetylene torch set off an explosion of the gas tank. The tank had been removed from the vehicle being repaired and placed a short distance away. The explosion caused the death of one pupil and serious injuries to the other. Ironically, the pupil operating the acetylene torch and doing the repair work received only minor injuries.

A judgment in the amount of $33,743 was made to a vocational school welding student who sustained injuries to his left hand and abdomen*(49)*. The plaintiff was observing the teacher as he attempted to cut the top off of a freon cylinder on an engine lathe. The cylinder exploded and the top portion struck the plaintiff causing the alleged injuries. Judgment was entered in favor of the plaintiff and the defendant state appealed, charging that the student was contributorily negligent. The higher court, in affirming the lower court decision, said the plaintiff was not contributorily negligent and the damages would stand.

An adult education welding course was the scene of an accidental injury resulting in an action to recover against the teacher and the board of education on the theory that the teacher had negligently permitted the student to weld without proper instructions*(50)*. The plaintiff was using welding equipment provided by the school district when an explosion occurred causing serious injury to the student. The trial court granted a motion to dismiss the complaint based on sovereign immunity and lack of statutory consent. The plaintiff appealed. The Court of Appeals held that

---

(48) Dutcher v. *City of Santa Rosa High School District,* 290 P.2d 316. California 1957.

(49) Danos v. *Foret, et al.*, 354 S.2d 667. Louisiana 1977.

(50) Salyers v. *Burkart,* 352 N.E.2d 156. Ohio 1974. And 339 N.E.2d 652. Ohio 1975.

the doctrine of sovereign immunity did apply to the Board but not to the teacher. The judgment was affirmed in part and reversed in part. It was further determined that evening or day schools for adults, out of school use, or technical schools and institutes for instruction beyond the high school are authorized activities for local boards. It concluded that there was no authority in Ohio which extends the cloak of governmental immunity to a teacher and that the general rule provides that teachers are individually liable for their own torts. The judgment of the trial court dismissing the complaint against the defendant was reversed and the case was remanded to the trial court for further proceedings pursuant to law.

Student participation in a questionable learning activity was the main issue in *Morris* v. *Ortiz*(51). Severe hand cuts were sustained by the plaintiff in the auto shop during an unsuccessful attempt by members of the class to bend an auto top that had been removed from an automobile. A claim of negligence was brought even though it was clearly established that the teacher was in close proximity at the time of the injury. The court ruled in favor of the teacher and concluded that the teacher could not have foreseen the injury-producing event nor could he have anticipated the actions of other members of the class. More specific details of this case can be found on page 21 of Chapter 2.

A California court found that failure on the part of a teacher to warn of the dangers involved in loading and firing a cannon was sufficient to constitute the proximate cause of an injury to a student(52). The teacher was declared negligent and the school district liable for payment of damages to the injured student. The ruling departs somewhat from the norm in that the injury-producing accident occurred after school hours and off of school property. Facts of the case reveal that the plaintiff had constructed a bronze scale model of a Revolutionary War-type cannon as a class project in the school machine shop. When completed, the student took the cannon home and into a shed behind his house. He then proceeded to dismantle a shotgun shell, setting the shot and powder aside. Next he muzzle-loaded the cannon, successively using the powder from the shotgun shell, rag wadding, the shot, and additional wadding. The student then mixed other powder with matchheads and worked this combination into the touch hole with a thin pointed instrument. Either simultaneously or within 10 seconds thereafter the cannon fired, blowing off two fingers from his hand and a portion of his palm and wrist.

---

(51) *Morris* v. *Ortiz*, 437 P.2d 652. Arizona 1968.

(52) *Calandri* v. *Ione Unified School District of Amador County*, 33 Cal Rptr. 333. California 1963.

Damage claims have been filed against teachers and school districts for student injuries resulting from accidents which have occurred in detached locations. If school-sponsored or related, responsibility follows the activity and extends beyond the boundaries of the school buildings proper. The principles of school law prevail even though the injury-producing accident may have occurred outside the physical confines of the school or in a peripheral area.

In a New Jersey case, action was brought for injuries sustained by a student while participating in the school's cooperative industrial education program(*53*). The cooperative program was a result of the Vocational Education Act of 1963. The plaintiff, a 17-year-old senior, was injured while working on the roof of a privately owned industrial building. The student lost his balance and fell to the ground while engaged in repairing the roof.

The board of education was held not liable for damages under the provisions of a State Court Claims Act. The court ruled that immunity provisions of the Tort Claims Act, in combination with case law delineating only minimal exceptions to reenactment of sovereign immunity for public entities, dictated the conclusion that the board was not liable for failure to supervise vocational activities conducted on the private property of the co-defendant. The defendant board moved for a summary judgment which was subsequently granted.

Court action resulted from an injury sustained by a student participating in a school-sponsored program under the egis of the Manpower Development and Training Act of 1962(*54*). The plaintiff allegedly suffered injuries while using machinery provided for use in the training program. In the complaint it was alleged that the school had provided dangerous and defective equipment and that the teacher had failed to adequately warn the plaintiff of the potential hazards involved.

The Superior Court sustained demurrers and the plaintiff appealed. The court held that neither the city nor the city school committee could be held liable for the alleged negligent acts of employees under the doctrine of *respondeat superior.* An order sustaining joint demurrers of the city school committee and agency was affirmed. However, negligence of the individual teacher was sufficient to state cause of action against the teacher. The order sustaining demurrer of the teacher was therefore reversed and the case remanded.

Common-law immunity was upheld in a case involving injury to a pu-

---

(*53*) *Cadmus* v. *Long Branch Board of Education,* 382 A.2d 98. New Jersey 1977.

(*54*) *Oeschger* v. *Fitzgerald,* 314 N.E.2d 444. Massachusetts, 1974.

pil in a woodworking shop(55). The pupil, while being instructed in the use of the planer by the teacher, attempted to remove the shavings which had accumulated and covered the blade of the planer. In doing so, the thumb of his right hand was caught in the ungarded planer and lacerated. The plaintiff alleged that failure to provide guards for the planer was in violation of the state code and constituted a nuisance. The court, in deciding in favor of the school district, ruled that it did not constitute a nuisance and that the general rule of immunity of school districts applied.

The board of education was absolved of liability on the point of law of proximate cause in a case resulting from an injury to a pupil on a jigsaw(56). The pupil sustained injuries to his finger when it was caught and mangled in the belt-drive mechanism of the jigsaw. The parents of the pupil charged that the board of education was negligent in failing to provide a safety guard. The injury occurred when a second pupil, in violation of known safety practices, turned on the saw while the plaintiff was cleaning it. The court ruled that the act of the second pupil was an independent, intervening act which broke the chain of causation between the accident and the alleged negligence, and thereby became the proximate cause of the accident. It was established that the shop teacher had conducted and maintained an adequate safety program.

Although the initial action against a school board to recover damages for injuries sustained during a shop class was of prime concern, the decision in *Scott* v. *School Board of Granite School District*(57) had as its major concern the plaintiff's failure to comply with statutes requiring that notice be given of claims against school districts in a specified manner. Action was brought as a result of an injury to the plaintiff while the plaintiff was in the process of changing a drive belt on a drill press and a fellow student turned on the power. The injury resulted in amputation and the action was filed. A summary judgment in favor of the school district was handed down by the lower court which was subsequently vacated by the higher court. The decision was therefore set aside and the case remanded for further proceedings.

The principle *res ipsa loquitur* was invoked in a California decision awarding an injured student $60,000(58). The student was involved in a

---

(55) *Golish* v. *School District of Borough of Windber,* 15 Som. 125. Pennsylvania 1950.

(56) *Meyer* v. *Board of Education,* 86 A.2d 761. New Jersey 1952.

(57) *Scott* v. *School Board of Granite School District,* 568 P.2d 746. Utah 1977.

(58) *Furtado* v. *Montebello Unified School District,* 23 Cal. Rptr. 476. California 1962.

series of mishaps culminating in the amputation of one leg above the knee. Initially, the student had bruised his foot running barefoot on the school track. Some months later surgery was performed on the foot and the student returned to school on crutches with his foot bandaged. In metals class, the teacher inadvertently dropped a steel bar on the bandaged foot. The student returned to the hospital for additional surgery, eventually resulting in the removal of the leg because of cancer.

California and New York traditionally have more cases of court record resulting from school shop accidents than other states. This may be explained in part because in California suits are brought directly against the district. This is one of the few states in which school districts have legal responsibility for accidents that involve pupils while they are participating in school activities. Under the California statute, a plaintiff may recover by proving either: the existence of danger known to authorities and failure to guard pupils against it; or an unknown peril, which by exercise of ordinary care, a reasonably prudent person would have discovered. New York school districts can be sued for damages resulting from accidents in the public schools because of the abrogation of governmental immunity by statute (see chapter 4).

Shop Accidents Not Litigated

The specific nature of injuries and the actual number of accidents occurring in school shops is difficult to ascertain. This is primarily because many accidents are not reported and, secondly, because there is no central agency to record these accidents on a state or national level. The school-shop accidents surveyed here point up the seriousness of the problem and indicate the need for accurate reporting.

The following account of a school-shop accident received limited publicity. A suit was not brought, although the accident was of a serious nature and resulted in the death of a junior high school pupil. The pupil involved had attached a tabletop 36 inches in diameter to the face of a small woodturning bench-type lathe. The lathe, in turn, was secured to the top of the bench near one end. The pupil's intention was to sand and polish the tabletop while it was turning on the lathe, thereby making a smoother surface and a higher quality product. He was instructed by the shop teacher to run the lathe at the lowest speed possible. To make certain that the lathe was set properly, the teacher adjusted the lathe speed himself. He even started the lathe and let it run to satisfy himself that it was operating properly and running at low speed. However, when the teacher had gone on to assist other pupils in the class, the pupil switched the lathe to the highest speed possible. This resulted in an extremely high rpm, causing the tabletop to fly apart and kill the boy.

In analyzing this accident, several important factors are evident. The teacher seemingly did all he could to prevent the tragedy. He gave proper instructions, set the lathe at the desired speed, and even turned it on to assure himself that it was operating properly. A tachometer check of the lathe was made by the coordinator of the school following the accident. It was concluded that, had the boy followed instructions, the tragedy could have been averted.

In another school-shop accident, for which a lawsuit was filed but subsequently settled out of court, the school district, the superintendent of schools, the school board, the director of the vocational school, two instructors, and a pupil were involved. Details of the accident indicate that two pupils in an aeronautics class were testing an aircraft engine mounted on a testing frame. The pupils involved were cranking the engine by hand, with one turning the propeller while the other was at the controls. The controls included the throttle and a switch. The pupils alternated between spinning the propeller and handling the controls. Following an exchange of positions, the engine started and ran at high speed as if the throttle were wide open. The pupil spinning the propeller had also set the throttle and switch. The engine and the stand it was mounted on commenced to move forward; the student who had just spun the propeller moved backward. The student moving backward, however, was struck by the spinning propeller and fatally injured. An attempt to render first aid was of no avail.

Both pupils had had previous experience and instruction in the procedures involved. For one reason or another, the stakes which normally held the stand down were not anchored according to the instructions as they had been previously. The plaintiff's attorney drew up a complaint charging carelessness, recklessness, and negligence on the part of the defendants as being the proximate cause of death. After several hearings and considerable discussion, the case was settled out of court. The insurance company, which provided insurance for the school district, paid the damages.

This accident was unusual in that it occurred in a vocational school, with the participants being more mature than average high school pupils. The responsibility for this accident would be difficult to assign unless it were possible to determine who was supposed to anchor the stakes holding the stand on which the engine was mounted and who was responsible for checking to see that the stakes were anchored. Since no mention was made at the time as to the condition of the stakes, it must be assumed that they were in working order and adequate. If they were, and it would seem likely that at least some of the responsibility for anchoring the stakes would fall to the pupils working on that particular engine, the injured pupil could be said to have been contributorily negligent for his own death. The pupil himself assumes some degree of risk when he enters an aeronautics class in which a degree of hazard is involved. If the teacher, foreseeing the consequences of not having the stakes anchored, did not insist that they be anchored, he could have been negligent, with this being determined as the proximate cause of the injury to the pupil.

The following account of a school-shop accident appeared in a newspaper some years ago. The pupil was engaged in making a knife from a file in the machine shop. The knife had been completed and the pupil was attaching a handle to it when, in some unaccountable manner, he slipped and fell. As he fell, the knife entered his left side, piercing his left ventricle. The pupil reported the accident to others in the room, stating that he had cut himself. He was rushed to the hospital, but the loss of blood had so weakened him that, even after a blood transfusion from his brother, death ensued a few hours after the accident.

The facts of this accident raise the question of allowing a potentially hazardous object to be constructed in a school shop, even though the operations involved in its construction might fulfill some objectives of the course. The responsibility of project selection and control should rest primarily with the teacher. If the teacher could not, or did not, foresee the possible danger involved, it might be said that he was negligent through the lack of foreseeability. Pupils of junior and senior high school age are not always aware of the potential danger that may be inherent in the construction of a particular object.

A more recent school-shop accident claimed a pupil's life but was not litigated. The pupil's coveralls caught fire from an acetylene torch he was using as a regular, scheduled part of his shop work. The pupil was wearing greasy coveralls and before the teacher and other members of the class could remove them, he was severely burned. He was removed to the hospital and died shortly thereafter. The administration stated that they did not feel that the teacher had been negligent in this instance.

In interpreting the cause of this accident and the assignment of responsibility for it, several factors must be considered. If the torch was being used in a negligent or careless manner after thorough and complete instructions by the teacher, the pupil himself could share in the responsibility. If the teacher had failed to thoroughly instruct the pupil in all phases of the use of the torch and, furthermore, had failed to insist that all safety precautions be followed, he might be considered negligent. The related fact that the pupil was wearing, and was permitted to wear, greasy coveralls might emphasize that proper safety precautions were not being followed.

Instruction on and use of the acetylene torch is accepted as a bona fide learning experience for qualified students. Specific controls and the enforcement of given regulations are necessary to maintain an orderly learning process and to protect students from injury. This is particularly important in the early stages of acquiring skills on an unfamiliar machine or piece of equipment. Students on occasion become overconfident and make value judgments not in the best interests of their own or their fellow students' health and welfare. A situation of this nature occurred in a midwestern school but fortunately did not result in personal injury. Contrary to the instructions of the teacher, the student took an empty gasoline drum into the vocational agriculture workshop and began cutting the top with an acetylene torch. The resultant explosion blew the top against the ceiling, shattered 27 windows, and scattered debris over the shop. Miraculously, the torch operator and three other students escaped injury.

Accidents can happen in the school shop as a result of regular procedures, either acceptable or borderline. A procedure, which was formerly used quite extensively but is now looked on with disfavor, is the use of denatured alcohol for the purpose of bringing out or raising the grain of wood. In one instance, two pupils were using alcohol from a five-gallon can for this purpose. An explosion took place, badly burning the two boys. Facts of the accident indicate that at the time of the explosion there were about three gallons of alcohol left in the can. The can used was the same container that the alcohol had come in from the manufacturer and it had only one small opening in the top. About 30 seconds prior to the explosion, the teacher had been standing near the two boys and talking with them. He started to walk to the other end of the classroom to assist other pupils when the explosion took place. The exact cause of the explosion is unknown. After the explosion, the resulting fire was extinguished, and everything conceivable was done to bring relief to the injured pupils.

In reviewing the facts of this accident, it was evident that a flammable material was being used with the knowledge of the teacher. If a teacher allows materials of this nature to be used without proper instructions and precautions, he might be considered negligent.

The absence of, or the misuse of, guards on power equipment in the school shop contributes to the number of school accidents each year. One example of this is a pupil who was injured on an unguarded circular saw. While engaged in the work required in the wood shop, the pupil had to saw a piece of wood. In so doing, his left hand came into contact with the saw, cutting off one-half of his thumb, two-thirds of his first finger, and all of his second finger. As a result, he lost the greater part of the use of his left hand and will suffer thereafter for the remainder of his life. The parents of the injured pupil claimed that he was injured as a result of failure to have the equipment guarded. Legal action in this case was averted because the state attorney general ruled that governmental immunity of the school district was in force.

It was pointed out that the saw could have been provided with a guard sufficient to render it safe for use by young, inexperienced pupils. Soon after this accident, a guard was placed on the saw by the school authorities. Negligence here was implied by the installation of a guard on the saw. In view of the facts of this case, it might be interpreted that if the injured pupil and his parents had brought action against the teacher, there might have been a better chance of obtaining a judgment. It must be remembered that even though the school board and the school district are protected by governmental immunity, the teacher may not be.

A high school boy was the victim in an unusual accident involving a wood lathe and a lathe tool. The boy was turning a bowl when the lathe tool hit an imperfection in the wood, throwing the handle of the lathe tool into the boy's abdomen. There was no bloody wound, not even a puncture. However, the boy developed a severe pain in his abdomen and was taken to the hospital. Paralysis of the intestines developed and he died six days later.

An unusual aspect of this accident was the fact that the boy was evidently performing a required operation in a legitimate manner. Whether or not the wood was inspected prior to use to be sure it was free of imperfections is not known. It can be assumed that the pupil was satisfied with the material before mounting it on the lathe. The position in which the boy was standing while at work on the lathe would also be of some importance. Another consideration would be the method by which he was holding the lathe tool. These mechanical practices would be an outcome of the instructions given by the teacher on the proper methods of wood turning.

Extraneous objects, equipment, or materials brought into the classroom have been causation factors in student injuries and, on occasion, death. Such was the case in a private eastern academy where a 14-year-old student was killed and the instructor and eight other students injured when a 40mm artillery shell exploded in the industrial arts classroom. The force of the explosion blew out the windows of the classroom and embedded shell fragments in the walls. The shell, found on an Army base near the school, had been brought into the classroom by one of the students in the class. It was anticipated that certain portions of the shell would be used in fashioning an ashtray. Attempts were being made to open the shell by drilling when the explosion occurred.

This accident differs from the norm in that it could have been predicted with a high degree of certainty. An nondefused artillery shell is inherently dangerous. Artillery shells are designed as explosive devices for the specific purpose of doing harm. The instructor apparently vacated his responsibility in not insisting on the removal of the shell by the proper authorities without delay. Nonetheless, at least one student was allowed to drill on the casing with tragic results. Negligence by reason of lack of foreseeability could be a distinct possibility.

Summary

The laws governing the operation of public schools are based primarily on state statutes and judicial opinions, with the structural pattern of education and the mode of its operation determined by constitutional provisions, statutory enactments, and judicial decisions. Public education is recognized as a function of the state, but the actual business of educating the children rests largely with the local school district.

Teaching personnel in the public school are governed by certain divisions of the law which relate directly or indirectly to the function of the public school system. If a state does not have statutes which are designed particularly to cover the aspect of liability resulting from pupil accidents, that state is considered to be under the jurisdiction of the common-law principle of immunity.

Recent years have witnessed an upsurge in the number of school-related statutory enactments, federal legislation, and court decisions. These legal enactments and subsequent interpretations are having a far-ranging influence on the lives of all who are directly, and even indirectly, associated with public education, including students, parents, teachers, supervisors, and members of boards of education.

The common-law principle of governmental immunity is basically that school districts are not liable to pupils and their parents for injuries resulting from the negligence of their teachers. A state legislature may abrogate the common-law principle by statute, but in order to hold a school district liable, the statute must expressly make it liable and do so in clear and concise terms. Court decisions have generally upheld the principle of governmental immunity and have decreed that no school district can accept liability voluntarily and waive its immunity, since a school district is a subordinate unit without the power to make itself liable.

The status of the doctrine of governmental immunity remains one of the most unsettled questions of law as it relates to teacher and school district liability. The view prevails in support of the doctrine that school funds are trust funds which have been set aside for the sole purpose of maintaining the school and cannot be diverted to other purposes. Attempts have been made to develop legal principles that will serve as guides in analyzing future educational situations and making sound judgments. Rather than abrogating governmental immunity, some states have created a state claims board to investigate claims and pay damages which result from the activities of governmental subdivisions and their employees.

Most school districts operate within the framework of governmental immunity. This condition makes teachers of shop subjects extremely vulnerable to charges of negligence. Public school teachers have no special immunity because they are public employees, or because of their position. Moreover, they freely accept the personal responsibility of due care toward the pupils under their care and direction.

Public school teachers assume some of the rights and duties of the parents in a school situation under the principle of *in loco parentis*. This can be summarized as the principle of the power of the school to control the conduct of the pupils and can be regarded as the legal duty of teachers to care for school children. This principle does not in any way relieve the teacher of liability, because every person owes an obligation to act or to use that which he controls in such a manner as to prevent injury to others.

School administrators, teachers, parents, and the general public dread having a school pupil involved in an accident. This concern is not only from the standpoint of the personal well-being of the pupils, but also from the standpoint of the legal complications which may develop should a school accident result in litigation.

In general, claims against public school teachers will not be upheld in court unless it can be shown that the injury occurred because they exceeded their authority, used poor judgment, or, for other reasons, failed to take reasonable precautions, resulting in a charge of negligence. Teachers do not attempt to guarantee that no injuries or damages will result from their acts. It is important to realize that it is only damages caused by negligent action that subject teachers to legal liability for damages.

If shop teachers are subject to liability for injuries to pupils, it may be expected that they will hesitate to make use of some of the educational tools and machines that require manipulation on the part of the pupils. Although a teacher may not be held liable for pupil injuries unless it can be proved that he was negligent, there are far-reaching implications of liability involved. It would seem logical that in a state which by statute allows the school district to assume liability for injuries, injured pupils and their parents would be less likely to bring suit against the individual teacher.

Review Questions

1. What are the primary sources of school law? How can these affect teacher liability?
2. What governmental body has the authority to enact statutes?
3. Under what conditions can an individual shop teacher be held liable for a pupil injury in the school shop?
4. How does the potential liability of a shop teacher compare with that of a mathematics teacher? With that of a chemistry teacher?
5. What importance is attached to the fact that teachers are classified as employees rather than officers?
6. What direct effect does the common-law immunity of school districts have on individual teacher liability? On the school district?
7. Why is the individual teacher not included under the principle of governmental immunity as are the school districts?
8. What modifications have been made in the doctrine of common-law immunity as applied to school districts? In which states? By what means?
9. What is the status of common-law immunity in your state? If it has been changed, what factors conditioned the change and what agencies were involved in the change?
10. In what way does the principle of governmental immunity affect the governing bodies of state colleges and universities?
11. What legal protection or benefit does an individual teacher derive from the principle of *in loco parentis?*
12. What effect do recorded court decisions have on present and future litigation?
13. In what ways can a thorough analysis of school-shop accidents, either litigated or not, assist a teacher in doing a better job of teaching?
14. What is the constitutionality of legislation placing a dollar limit on a school district's tort liability?

CHAPTER 4

Safeguarding Teachers from Litigation and Damage Claims

WHILE there is often considerable speculation as to whether or not a claim against a teacher can be sustained, court records indicate that many cases involving alleged negligence of the teacher have been litigated as noted in the preceding chapter. It is an established principle of law that an individual who has been negligent can be held legally liable for injuries to others. Public school teachers in general, and shop teachers in particular, are classified as individuals in tort actions and are thereby subject to suit resulting from their negligent actions.

Experience shows that accidents do occur despite modern safety devices and seemingly adequate safety instructions. In view of this, and because teachers have been sued as a result of school accidents, several methods which aim to relieve the teacher of the burden of paying judgments have been explored and, in some instances, put into effect. Paramount among these are:

1. Modification of the nonliability principle as applied to school districts.
2. Progressive legislation relieving teachers of liability.
3. Group liability insurance through state and national education associations or teachers' unions.
4. Personal liability insurance acquired on an individual basis.
5. Legal services provided by the local school district or by local and state education associations.

Individual states differ not only in the type of legislation that has been enacted, but also in its interpretation. When it comes to the legal assessment, certain distinctions are drawn. Teachers and other school employees, unlike the district which employs them, do not always enjoy immunity from tort liability. In the majority of states, the individual teacher receives no special legal protection by virtue of the appointed position, although the school district, as a governmental subdivision, is often protected by the principle of common-law immunity. In most cases, the teacher is not only unwilling, but usually unable, to meet the financial burden of a lawsuit. These factors reinforce the teacher's need for assistance and protection should an accident occur.

Legislation

In view of the precarious position that the teacher occupies with regard to liability resulting from classroom accidents, teachers' associations are expressing an interest in legislation which may serve to relieve the situation. Several states have passed such legislation and similar legislation is pending or under consideration in several other states. It does not seem possible, however, under the provisions of the U.S. Constitution to fully relieve public school teachers from liability for the negligence of their acts while teaching. Although this area of law would have to be tested by court action, it might be against public policy to enact what could be construed as class legislation. This remains true in spite of an increasing number of lawsuits involving teachers and schools, pointing up the need for enlightened legislation. Legislation absolving teachers of any liability resulting from pupil accidents in the school was unsuccessfully attempted by the 1957 Nebraska Legislature.

Some states have statutes that directly impose liability on the school district. Actions of this type are governed by the provisions of the statutes allowing the school district to assume liability. This in itself is not the ultimate in the evolution of responsibility for school accidents, because a school district may be called on to assume an unexpected and substantial judgment under a statute of this kind. This was true in *Welch* v. *Dunsmuir Joint Union High School District*(*1*), where suit was brought against a California school district because of a football injury. Medical testimony showed that the plaintiff was a permanent quadriplegic because of damage to his spinal cord. Judgment was obtained in favor of the plaintiff in the amount of $325,000. On request of the trial court, and because of the

(*1*) *Welch* v. *Dunsmuir Joint Union High School District,* 326 P.2d 633. California 1958.

financial hardship imposed on the school district, the plaintiff agreed to a reduction of the damages assessed to $206,804. Recently, damage claims in excess of one million dollars have become commonplace.

The state of Hawaii displayed a degree of progressiveness when it passed the Tort Liability Act of 1957 (Act 312-S.B. 892). Under the provisions of this act, a teacher, as an individual, is not liable if sued for actions within the scope of his employment. Such a suit is brought against the government agency with legal counsel provided by the attorney general's office. Court costs, attorney's fees, and any judgment rendered will be assumed by the government.

Abrogation of Immunity

The common-law rule of governmental immunity as applied to school districts, as noted previously, prevails in all states where it has not been abrogated by statutory authorization or supreme court decision. The purchase of liability insurance by a school district does not in itself result in abrogation of immunity even to the extent of the insurance. The abrogation or revocation of common-law immunity of school districts normally requires legislative or supreme court action.

Recognizing that the legislative process required to abrogate the common-law immunity of school districts is gradual, some courts have not waited and have taken exception to the doctrine. An analysis of selected judicial opinions indicates that modern courts do not apply the doctrine of nonliability as often as in the past. This is particularly true when to do so would impose undue hardship on the injured party(*2*).

As pointed out in the preceding chapter, the common law of school districts has been abrogated or modified in several states by legislation and, more recently, by action of the supreme court. States that have succeeded in statutorily abrogating common-law immunity include: California, Connecticut, Iowa, New York, Oklahoma, Oregon, Utah, and Washington. Hawaii can also be included in this group because of the passage of the Tort Liability Act. The legislatures in South Carolina and Texas have made certain modifications in the law that particularly affect school district liability. States which have succeeded in rejecting the principle of common-law immunity by supreme court decision include: Alaska, Arizona, Colorado, Florida, Idaho, Illinois, Indiana, Kentucky, Louisiana, Michigan, Minnesota, Missouri, Nebraska, Nevada, New Jersey,

---

(*2*) *Sawaya* v. *Tucson High School District No. 1 of Pima County,* 281 P.2d 105. Arizona 1955.

Pennsylvania, Rhode Island, Wisconsin, and the District of Columbia. California permits suits against school districts for injury caused by the negligence of their employees. Connecticut and New York also have enacted legislation which allows school funds to be used in payment of damages arising out of injury to pupils through the alleged negligence of their employees. Washington, after passing common-law immunity legislation, revised it to prohibit suits against school districts for accidents that occur in physical education and industrial education. Although this revision was first passed in 1917, it still holds true(*3*).

It must be emphasized that even though a school district is made liable by statute, the teacher is not relieved of personal liability. A teacher can be joined in a suit and can be held liable. There have been cases of liability brought jointly against the teacher and the school district in which the teacher was held liable and the school district declared immune. An example of this would be *DeGooyer* v. *Harkness*(*4*) in South Dakota. Although this case did not involve a shop accident, the principle of law aplied was the same.

Save-Harmless Legislation

The legislatures of a few states have passed laws requiring or permitting school districts to reimburse employees who are held liable for injuries resulting from negligence. These are called "save-harmless" laws and, when in force, provide that each school district shall protect and save its employees from financial harm incurred during the course of assigned school duties. According to the interpretation of these laws, the school district will pay the damages only if the negligent act complained of was one that the employee undertook while acting in the due course of his employment.

Save-harmless laws either require or permit school districts to pay the costs of any lawsuit or judgments teachers may suffer as a result of negligence in their positions. It has been maintained by many persons that this is sound legislation and that teachers' associations in all states should take steps to urge the enactment of such legislation. In addition, it is felt that save-harmless statutes should be mandatory not merely permissive. This would mean, in effect, that the school districts would not have a choice in the matter, but would be compelled to assist financially any teacher who

---

(*3*) *Babcock* v. *School District No. 17 of Clallam County*, 358 P.2d 547. Washington 1961.

(*4*) *DeGooyer* v. *Harkness*. 13 N.W.2d 815. South Dakota 1944.

has been sued because of alleged negligence while carrying out his assigned school duties.

At least six states have enacted variations of save-harmless legislation affecting public school teachers. A Wyoming statute *empowers or permits* the school districts to come to the aid of teachers who are found liable in damages for injuries resulting from their negligence. In Connecticut, Iowa, Maine, New Jersey, and New York, statutes *require* the school districts to assist teachers.

Unsuccessful attempts were made in 1959 by the Oregon and Idaho Education Associations to obtain save-harmless legislation in their respective states. In Oregon, opposition was mainly from attorneys who were members of the state legislature. They expressed reluctance to pass legislation which protects only teachers. It was felt that it would be construed as class legislation since it was not specifically designed to include all other civil employees of the state.

The Idaho Education Association had made several previous attempts to enact this legislation without success. However, in 1959 the Idaho Legislature did pass what is referred to as the Idaho "waiver law." While complete save-harmless protection is not afforded by this statute, it can be achieved if all school districts purchase liability insurance and include their employees by specific endorsement on the policy. Other aspects of this statute are discussed under the section on insurance in this chapter.

In most states the enactment of a save-harmless statute does not make the school district liable for the teacher's negligence although the district can be held liable for the *damages* assessed as a result of the teacher's negligence. An exception to this is the state of New York where school districts have been obligated to save the teachers harmless since the enactment of Section 3923 of the Education Law of 1953. The New York save-harmless law was enacted in 1937 for school districts and extended in 1953 to cover all employees of school districts with less than one million pupils. The New York courts have interpreted the save-harmless law as, in effect, imposing direct liability on the school district, saying that it was unnecessary to sue an employee and obtain a judgment before seeking settlement of the judgment from the school district. New York has abolished the precept of nonliability and the liability of schools rests on the presence of negligence on the part of the teacher. School districts in the state can take out insurance against such liability or, in qualified situations, act as self-insurers.

Save-harmless legislation is perhaps the most complete in New York and New Jersey. In 1961, the New York legislature demonstrated foresight when it extended the provisions of the statute to protect student or practice teachers, as well as the regular staff, against financial loss. In 1977, the New Jersey legislature broadened their statute provisions to "include any student teacher or person assigned to other professional pre-training field experience for any act or ommission arising out of and in the course of the performance of the duties of such office, position, employment, or student teaching or other assignment to professional field experience"(5). Under these provisions, the school board is required to defray all costs of defending against an action, including reasonable counsel fees and expenses and the cost of appeals, if any, and shall save harmless and protect such person from any financial loss resulting therefrom.

In other states which have enacted save-harmless legislation, the school district is not held liable for the employee's negligence but is obligated to protect the employee from financial loss. Although New Jersey enacted a save-harmless law in the same year as New York, courts in that state held that direct action against a school district was not possible. New Jersey and Connecticut save-harmless laws include officers and board members as well as all employees in the school district. On the other hand, Wyoming laws protect only teachers and members of the supervisory and administrative staff. In a Connecticut case involving assault and battery(6), the superior court of record held that a save-harmless statute did not have the effect of abolishing the common-law rule of governmental immunity from liability.

In the review and analysis of save-harmless laws as applied to education, several very significant facts stand out. Basically, these statutes serve as protection to teachers in the event that a pupil is injured while participating in a class activity. Save-harmless legislation also has tremendous value in its ability to provide a degree of security for the individual teacher, to reduce the number of judgments obtained against school districts based on the alleged negligence of the teacher, and to lower the sums which they may be called on to pay. Even though these laws may permit or require a school district to supply or pay for an employee's legal defense, the school district's governmental immunity from liability is generally upheld. Normally the plaintiff's most reasonable recourse is against the individual teacher who can turn to the school district to pay any damages resulting from an adverse judgment.

---

(5) *New Jersey Code Amended,* 18A; 16-6, 1977.

(6) *Swainback* v. *Coombs,* 115 A.2d 468. Connecticut 1955.

Safe-Place Statutes

Legislation requiring safe construction and proper maintenance of public buildings has been enacted in a few states. This legislation has resulted in the so-called "safe-place" statutes and although they pertain to public buildings in general they do not always include school buildings. The Wisconsin safe-place statutes do include school buildings, however, and provide that every public building shall be so constructed as to render it safe. These statutes then permit suit for injuries against school districts when the injury is the direct result of the school district's failure to construct, maintain, or keep its buildings in such a manner as to render them safe.

Safe-place statutes have been strictly interpreted by the courts as indicated in *Kirchoff* v. *City of Janesville*(7). A pupil was injured on an allegedly unguarded planer in the school wood shop and sued the city on the grounds that it had not provided a safe place for the operation of a dangerous machine. It was also claimed that safety devices and methods were inadequate and that the teacher had failed in his duty to provide instruction in the proper operation of a dangerous machine and to warn of the dangerous nature of the machine.

In finding for the school district, the court held that, although public buildings are subject to the safe-place statutes, these statutes did not apply to school shops. The court also ruled that the pupil was injured not because of an unsafe condition in the school but by a machine in the school. Pupils are not classified as employees and the school shop is not classified as a place of employment, even though some of the products of a vocational school may be sold. Since the pupil was not injured in a place of employment, the statute requiring safety devices on dangerous machines did not apply. The common law of governmental immunity was, therefore, upheld and the city declared not liable.

Situations such as these point up the fact that safe-place coverage in many states is not only inadequate to protect pupils from injuries caused by defective construction, but it is also often obscured behind misinterpretation and misunderstandings of juries, courts, and school administrators. The school district's responsibilities are not always spelled out in this area of law. It is likely that the courts will construe the statute as narrowly as possible so as to prohibit or discourage suits, unless expressly and clearly within the coverage of the legislation.

---

(7) *Kirchoff* v. *City of Janesville,* 38 N.W.2d 698. Wisconsin 1949.

Statutes of Limitation

The statutes of limitation in effect in a few states are actually laws restricting the amount of time that may elapse between an accidental injury and the filing of a notice of claim or damage suit. A Hawaiian statute designates a two-year period for filing of claims after the claim accrues. New York and California statutes require the injured party, his parents, or legal guardian, to give notice of intent to bring suit within 90 days of the actual injury. Legislation enacted in Wisconsin in 1963 provides that an action founded in tort must be brought against the school district within 120 days of the action or damage causing the claim. The requirement in Washington is one year and in Nevada, six months. These statutes maintain a degree of flexibility in that they permit the filing of late notice within one year from the time of injury with court approval. Permission has been granted by courts to file late claims where circumstances have indicated that it would impose undue hardships on the injured if the courts held strictly to the law.

Statutes of limitation have been involved in several court cases which developed as a result of injuries to pupils in the school shop. In *Osborn* v. *Board of Education of Marathon Central School District No. 1 of Freetown*(8), the plaintiff sustained injuries while operating a drill press in the school shop. Both father and son asked the court for permission to file a late notice of claim. The court held that the lack of maturity of the injured pupil and the mental incapacity of the father, due to distressing home circumstances during and following the time of the accident, were sufficient reasons for both claimants to be allowed to file a late notice of claim. From an order granting such permission, the board of education appealed. The court, however, held that permission to both claimants to file a late notice of claim was properly granted. The delay in filing the pupil's claim was excusable on the grounds of infancy. The emotional and mental distress of the father due to his wife's illness at the time of the injury, her subsequent death two weeks later, and the attendant burdens of home and job, constituted mental incapacity within the meaning of the statute for which cause the filing of a late notice of claim is provided.

In other cases involving statutes of limitation(9), the court held that the notice of claim was not timely. In ruling in favor of the defendant

---

(8) *Osborn* v. *Board of Education of Marathon Central School District No. 1 of Freetown,* 172. N.Y.S.2d 453. New York 1958.

(9) *Sigman* v. *Board of Education New York City,* 97 N.Y.S.2d 302. New York 1950.

board of education, the court indicated that it could have extended the time limit to one year on the basis of fact that the injured was a minor, but it had no authority to accept the case more than four years after the incident. In this case, a vocational-high-school pupil was injured on a wood lathe June 14, 1945. The pupil sustained an injury to his left hand allegedly by reason of the failure of the teacher to properly instruct and supervise him in the use of the machine and its equipment. A claim was filed on the corporation counsel within the statutory limit, but no notice of claim was filed on the school board as required by law. In March 1946, court action was instituted but was discontinued because of failure to file the notice with the board of education. Notice was duly filed on the board of education in 1948, beginning a new action. This terminated in the court's decision in 1950 in favor of the board of education.

Statutes of limitation can be directly beneficial to both individual teachers and school districts by protecting them from fraudulent and obsolete claims. In a state which does not have statutes of limitation in effect, it is conceivable that a school pupil who is injured when still a minor could bring suit against alleged negligent parties on attaining legal age. It stands to reason that when a claim is filed within a reasonable time following an accident, the facts are more accurately recalled and a more just disposition can be rendered. Facts which lie dormant for a period of months, or even years, have a tendency to be distorted, misrepresented, and conditioned by an individual's personal feelings and association with the case.

Occupational Safety and Health Act

U.S. Public Law 91-596, the Williams-Steiger Occupational Safety and Health Act (OSHA), was signed into law in December 1970 with an effective date of April 28, 1971. The stated purpose of the act is "to insure so far as possible every working man and woman in the nation safe and healthful working conditions and to preserve our human resources." In addition to offering a unitary set of standards for the majority of U.S. workers, OSHA has succeeded in bringing together the job safety shelters that exist within federal jurisdiction. These include the safety provisions of the Walsh-Healey Public Contracts Act, the Fair Labor Standards Act, the Longshoremen's and Harbor Workers' Compensation Act, and the Contract Work Hours and Safety Standards Act.

The Secretary of Labor and the Occupational Safety and Health Review Commission are responsible for the administration and enforcement of the Act. The National Institute for Occupational Safety and Health has prime responsibility for research and related functions under the direction of the Secretary of Health and Human Services. The Secretary of Labor is responsible for both promulgating and enforcing job safety and health standards. Under the Act, each *employer* has a duty to provide each of his employees with employment and a place of employment which is free from recognized hazards causing, or likely to cause, death or serious physical harm. The employee has the specific duty of complying with safety and health standards, and all rules, regulations, and orders issued pursuant to the Act which are applicable to his own actions and conduct.

By definition, federal, state, and local government employees are specifically excluded from coverage under the Act. This would appear to set aside the OSHA regulations as they might apply to public school systems and state-supported colleges and universities, however, these institutions may be covered by equally effective requirements. Section 18 of the Act provides a convenient aperture for potential coverage of state and local government employees.

Section 18 is concerned with state jurisdiction and state plans. Subsection (a) of Section 18 states: "Nothing in this Act shall prevent any state agency or court from asserting jurisdiction under state law over any occupational safety or health issue with respect to which no standard is in effect under Section 6." Subsection (c) of Section 18 and the subsequent subsection (6) read as follows;

> (c) The Secretary shall approve the plan submitted by a State under sub-section (b), or any modification thereof, if such plan in his judgment . . .
>
> (6) contains satisfactory assurances that such State will, to the extent permitted by its law, establish and maintain an effective and comprehensive occupational safety and health program applicable to all employees of public agencies of the State and its political subdivisions, which program is as effective as the standards contained in an approved plan.

Section 17 of that Act provides severe penalties for violations. Subsection (a) provides that any employer who willfully or repeatedly violates the act may be assessed a civil penalty of not more than $10,000 for each violation. Subsection (e) provides that an employer who commits a willful violation of the Act which causes death shall, if convicted, be punishable by a fine of not more than $10,000 or by imprisonment for not more than six months, or both. Employers are now subject to fine if they are not in compliance with specific standards, even if lack of compliance is not willful. Furthermore, OSHA officers must issue citations for lack of compliance even if the employer was uninformed of the standard violation and offers to correct it.

OSHA provides that individual states may assume responsibility for administration of their own occupational safety and health plans provided the plans have been approved by the Secretary of Labor. To be acceptable, state plans must be equal to or stronger than the federal law. Such plans must contain assurances that the individual states will establish and maintain an effective and comprehensive occupational safety and health program applicable to all employees of public agencies of the state and its political subdivisions.

It was expected that many state plans would be formulated and approved as early as December 1973. Within five years of the passage of OSHA, approximately 50% of the states had state OSHA plans approved by the Secretary of Labor. A slowing trend followed and few state plans were approved in the succeeding five years. After a state plan receives approval, OSHA retains enforcement authority for an evaluation period of at least three years. Presently, a three-phase evaluation procedure to measure the effectiveness of state plans is under development. In phase one, the refinements needed to distinguish an operational plan from a developmental plan will be worked out. In the second phase, continued evaluations will be made to decide on the final relinquishment of federal enforcement authority. Phase three will include further evaluation to ensure maintenance of a required level of effectiveness.

Although OSHA has been in effect since early in 1971, the full impact has not yet reached the public school system. Some incidental school inspections have been held with less than positive results. In the main, persons assigned to the state regulatory offices have been hard put to keep pace with required inspections of private business and industry. These inspections along with compiling of records, analysis of reports, and monitoring and evaluation of the program's efforts have taxed the physical resources of most state and local OSHA compliance offices. Until compliance coordinators meet the demands of business and industry, inspections of the local schools will not be common. Herein lies a rather serious problem. If school officials feel they are exempt by default, improvements are likely to be delayed or postponed indefinitely.

There is little doubt that many school shops, laboratories, cafeterias, and related facilities are presently in violation of the OSHA safety and health standards. Historically, teachers have assumed an attitude of immunity from personal responsibility but under the provisions of OSHA they will necessarily be involved. The sophisticated laboratory equipment and the attendant requirements of increased care and supervision require an awareness of the potential for liability claims. The immunities of yesteryear are slowly disappearing and the general rules of tort liability are increasingly applicable. Failure to comply with OSHA regulations could constitute negligence. A charge of negligence could be levied against a school district, a teacher, or both for (1) failure to require use of protection devices on machinery, (2) failure to comply with standards of personal protective equipment, and (3) failure to provide proper housekeeping in shops, classrooms, and laboratories.

Public schools are not yet a part of the normal inspection pattern of OSHA officials. A direct complaint, however, will result in a visit from the compliance coordinator. In one instance, a direct complaint brought about an inspection of a western metropolitan high school. The result was a list of more than 60 nonserious violations. Inspecting officials termed the violations common and stated that this school was typical. A nonserious citation is the mildest form of warning issued by compliance coordinators. Deficiencies listed by the OSHA official included (1) a lack of guard devices on power tools, (2) absence of power control devices on air hoses, and (3) storage of flammable liquids in open containers. The inspection team was particularly critical of saws, grinders, and lathes that did not have guards in place when being used by students in the school shops. In addition, worn cables were observed on the arc welding machine.

Literature pertaining to OSHA dwells primarily on its application to business and industry and excludes the schools. Educational institutions are rarely mentioned in the publications and only alluded to in state and governmental documents. It is no small wonder then that professional educators are confused as to the direct application of OSHA in educational institutions.

There is somewhat of a dichotomy with reference to compliance by public school systems and enforcement of provisions of the OSHA Act. All private schools are covered by federal or state safety and health standards. In those states where the federal government has not approved the states' enforcement of standards, public schools are not subject to any direct regulation under the OSHA Act. Attempting to interpret and apply to educational settings principles of safety that are written primarily for business and industry is fraught with danger and can lead to contradictions. There are definite differences in application and the degree to which compliance is possible. Business and industry generally involve adults while schools deal with youngsters in the formative stages of their lives, both physical and mental.

In the past, schools were very aware of their responsibility to provide a safe place to learn. Compliance became a matter of degree. With the passage of the Occupational Safety and Health Act, however, another ingredient has been added—health. Proper quality air control must also be addressed. Dust, fumes, and toxic gases must be controlled. A student with a respiratory ailment could easily compound the problem by breathing dust or fumes that had accumulated in a school shop or laboratory. Health and sanitation requirements go far beyond the traditional shop or laboratory safety program. In addition, noise exposure can cause permanent hearing damage and is perhaps one of the most commonly violated standards. The current maximum standard is 90 decibels.

There is genuine concern on the part of shop teachers regarding the breadth and depth of OSHA regulations as they apply to school situations. It appears to be only a matter of time before public school systems and state institutions of higher learning come under the egis of the law. It is conceivable that these governmental subdivisions will be included in some of the state plans. Schools will then be required to comply rigidly with the stated safety standards, recordkeeping requirements, and inspections. While many states have yet to consider legislation bringing educational facilities under the jurisdiction of OSHA regulations, the issue of the teacher's responsibility in implementing these regulations is of vital concern to all who teach vocational, industrial, and technical subjects. It is apparent that if OSHA is revised or modified, a chapter, section, or separate category should be created to deal directly with public education including universities, colleges, secondary, and elementary schools. To accomplish this task, active professional educators should be commissioned to determine the content. Public educational institutions have been slow to adopt the provisions of OSHA for a variety of reasons, including noninvolvement in the development of the Act. Reluctance to follow the provisions may in part be related to monetary restrictions. Of more immediate concern is the slowness to adopt the standards because of the confusion over responsibility and the realization that penalties may be slow in coming.

Whether or not a given state has ratified a state OSHA plan is often a moot point should legal action follow a student injury in the school shop. The prosecuting attorneys would be negligent of their duties if they did not lean heavily on the provisions of OSHA in establishing the standards of safety for school shops. Since most of the tools and machines utilized in the learning process are industrial in nature, it can easily be determined that guards and other safety devices are not only available but required by OSHA.

Insurance

Since public school teachers in most states receive little or no special legal consideration by reason of their position, the possibility of suit has brought about a growing interest in insurance protection. Teachers, usually financially unable to withstand the burden of a lawsuit, have purchased liability insurance in many instances as a method of protection against the risk of individual loss. Insurance has been referred to as a basic safety device and is considered a vital link in any well-proportioned safety program. The basic theory of insurance is to spread the risk over as wide an area as possible.

Humanitarian considerations require some provision for an innocent victim of an accidental injury. To meet this need, an acceptable insurance plan can provide a humane, effective, and, in the long run, economical answer to this and other closely allied problems. The purchase of liability insurance is usually up to the individual teacher or vested in the authority of the respective state. Although it is possible in a few states for the school district to purchase liability insurance for teachers, it is not a legal public expenditure in the majority of states.

Regarding the acquisition of liability insurance to cover school teachers, William L. Phinne, Attorney General for the State of New Hampshire, made the following ruling on January 3, 1950, as a result of a request by Milton C. Buley, Commissioner of Education:

> It is my opinion that a school district, although authorized to spend public funds to secure insurance, may not spend a school district's money for accident insurance to cover the individual liability of a school teacher. The school district and the school board are not liable for such accidents and the liability of the school teacher is a risk of employment which the individual teacher must cover, if he so desires.

In Minnesota, Attorney General Miles Lord handed down a decision regarding the purchase of liability insurance by a school district for its employees on August 10, 1955. This decision was in answer to a request by Dean M. Schweickhard, State Commissioner of Education. Mr. Lord ruled that a school board cannot spend money for liability insurance for its employees, including teachers, out of public funds. Lord also said the school board cannot spend money for general insurance coverage for school children while at school or for its school patrol.

This ruling by the Minnesota Attorney General was superseded by an act of the legislature which was approved March 8, 1957. This act provides that school districts may procure liability insurance covering school districts, officers, and employees of the school district. The waiver of the defense of governmental immunity made pursuant to such a provision in the insurance policy does not subject the city or school district to liability in excess of the insurance coverage provided by the policy.

Liability insurance is, in reality, an attempt to protect an individual against the need to personally pay judgments growing out of negligence. It is a contract or written agreement whereby the insurance company agrees to pay the damages for which the insured may be held liable and it is designed to limit the exposure of the insured. With respect to a school district carrying liability insurance, three alternatives are possible. First, common-law immunity is completely waived; second, immunity is waived to the extent of the insurance coverage; or third, the immunity is not waived at all.

The problem of liability insurance has plagued school districts for years, primarily conditioned by two opposing viewpoints. There are those who are captivated by the premise of governmental immunity and believe that the school district as a governmental body has no liability and that insurance against such liability is a misnomer, a waste, and possibly illegal. On the other hand, there are those who believe that because of the expansion of the curriculum in the public schools and the diversity of programs which have been introduced, the school district as a public body should accept some of the responsibility for liability. Legislation pertaining to this aspect of school law has been enacted in some states. An example is Connecticut, where the law allows the school district to spend public funds to insure liability with any insurance company authorized to write insurance in the state*(10)*. School districts may elect to act as self-insurers of such liability.

The 1950 Idaho Legislature passed a law which relates rather directly to liability insurance that may be carried by a school district. It is referred to as the Idaho "waiver law," and actually waives the immunity of the State of Idaho or other subdivisions against liability for damages to the extent of the liability insurance carried. Immunity above the amount of insurance carried is still maintained. School districts in Idaho are permitted, but not required, to purchase liability insurance. However, unless a rider specifies protection of the individual employee, the waiver of immunity still leaves the employees in hazard.

The courts have generally held that school districts are without the power to spend public funds for liability insurance unless a statute specifically permits it. Without statutory authorization, the practice of purchasing liability insurance for teachers and other employees by a school district is an *ultra vires* (act beyond the scope of authority) expenditure of school funds. If a school district has the authority to carry liability insur-

---

(10) *Connecticut Laws Relating to Education,* State Board of Education, Hartford 1950. Section 192.

ance on its teachers and other employees, it is recommended that a policy be obtained that gives injured parties adequate protection without having first to obtain a judgment against the school district. In states where school districts are allowed to purchase liability insurance to protect their teachers from damage claims resulting from pupil injuries, this insurance can be obtained from any insurance company registered with the state insurance department and handling that type of insurance.

Although some local school districts have taken it upon themselves to authorize the purchase of liability insurance despite governmental immunity, it is legally accepted that the most common authority by which school districts are granted permission to carry liability insurance for school-related pupil accidents is by state statute, through court decisions, or by an opinion of the attorney general. It must be appreciated, however, that even a state statute authorizing the purchase of insurance does not abrogate the common-law immunity of the school district. School districts and officials involved should follow a few basic recommendations with regard to the purchase of liability insurance. One of the first considerations is to establish the legality of the purchase before school district funds are expended. If insurance is allowed and is purchased by the school district, it must be adequate to safeguard the school district's funds and property against depletion by costly lawsuits and payment of resulting damages. In addition, it must be clear that any contract the school district enters into with an insuring company is not in conflict with existing state statutes and actually provides the protection that is necessary in a given situation.

In lieu of, or in addition to, liability insurance for teachers, some schools require, or make available to the pupils, accident insurance plans at a nominal rate. This type of plan is often handled by the school activities association, with the total cost payable by the pupil.

Group Liability Insurance

Liability insurance plans of a group nature are being accepted by educators as an equitable means of protection against the possibility of a judgment. Group insurance from a reliable company can be a reasonable, economical, and satisfactory investment.

The American Industrial Arts Association and the American Vocational Association have both participated in minimal premium Professional Liability Insurance Plans. The initial AIAA plan was in effect from July 1962 until November 1971, when it was discontinued. Enrollment in the plan never realized the potential anticipated and the insuring agency was forced to withdraw from the program. After several years of dormancy, however, the program was reactivated and this service is once again provided to the membership. Currently, the American Industrial Arts Association and the American Vocational Association offer comparable professional liability protection plans(*11*). These plans are available on application through the national offices of each organization. Each plan provides protection of up to $500,000 per occurrence or a $500,000 aggregate during any member's contract period. In addition, each plan provides protection for members while supervising student teachers in assigned professional activities. This means that the provisions of the plan cover the members for actions of their students while under their direct supervision. Student members, who choose to participate, are protected with the same provisions as professional members during their student teaching assignment.

Teachers' associations in approximately 47 states offer group liability insurance plans for all members. This liability insurance is most often included automatically as part of the yearly dues. Occasionally, however, payment of a nominal premium is required. In those states where the cost of the policy is included in the yearly association dues, the standard amount of protection provided is usually $1,000,000. Plans in specific states may vary somewhat from this standard. In Oregon, for example, two almost parallel plans are in effect. While the majority of teachers in the state are covered by a liability policy with a limit of $1,000,000, a small group of teachers in Portland is covered under a separate policy. In addition to teachers, the group in Portland includes school district administrators and members of the high school and elementary school principals' associations.

In Ohio, a group liability plan sponsored by the Ohio Industrial Arts Association was discontinued after two years because of lack of interest and participation. This coverage was offered on the basis of a master policy issued to the Ohio Industrial Arts Association by Lloyds of London. The policy was handled and serviced by an Ohio insurance company and included protection against judgment for corporal punishment of pupils and medical payments. The cost per member teacher per year was $7.95. The Ohio Education Association now offers $1,000,000 of liability protection through the Educator's Employment Liability program (EEL).

The plan now in effect in the state of Michigan is an example of an EEL program. Group liability insurance, sponsored by the Michigan Education Association since September 1954, was originally available

---

(*11*) Valid in all states except Texas. Professional liability protection is available in Texas through the Educator's Employment Liability program offered by the state teachers' association.

only through the Michigan Industrial Education Society. Now, all teachers who are members of the education association are covered by a $1,000,000 liability policy. When a teacher pays the normal yearly dues to the association, insurance is automatically included. It has been found that a single policy made out to the state association and covering all professional members reduces overhead to the point where the association can absorb the premiums as a service to each member.

The insuring agreement of the Michigan Education Association, which is representative of this type of insurance, states in part that the insurance company agrees to pay up to $1,000,000 which the insured might become obligated to pay, for damages resulting from bodily injury sustained by any person in an accident caused by personal acts arising in the course of duties as an employee of a board of education. The policy covers payment for the defense of an individual member in a suit for damages even if such suit is groundless, false, or fraudulent.

In Minnesota, if a member teacher of the state education association is held liable because of his actions, or his failure to act, in cases of injury, sickness, or death of a pupil, the group liability policy in force would pay defense suit costs including lawyer fees and court costs, judgments imposed by the courts, premiums on required bonds, and all other reasonable expenses incurred by the insured, other than wages, up to $1,000,000. To be covered, the teacher must be a current member of the Minnesota Education Association and be under contract to a board of education. The policy covers only school activities and no coverage is afforded while the teacher is operating or riding in a motor vehicle.

In addition to group liability plans sponsored by the state education associations, several states have related plans. In Connecticut, the vocational schools are state operated and all instructors are state employees and therefore are covered by the group liability policy handled by the state comptroller's office. Group liability insurance plans are also available through the American Federation of Teachers.

There are certain restrictions in regard to the liability insurance policies sponsored by some state associations. In Delaware, for example, shop teachers and physical education teachers are excluded from provisions of the state group policy when they attempt to administer first aid to pupils. Group liability protection is not possible for all teachers because of state insurance department disapproval in a few states. This prohibits the state teachers' associations in these states from offering a group liability policy for their member teachers.

Personal or Individual Liability Insurance

In those states where teachers are not protected by the means already discussed, they can investigate the possiblity of securing some form of individual liability insurance that would protect them against claims. Although the premise has been advanced that if teachers take out insurance it is an admission of liability, records have shown that shop teachers have been named in suits whether or not they were insured.

Individual liability policies are available in all states regardless of whether group liability coverage or save-harmless statutes are provided. There is no question as to the legality of a shop teacher purchasing liability insurance out of his own funds. It is possible for an individual teacher under public liability coverage to insure against any damage suit in which bodily injury, sickness, or death of a pupil is attributed to his negligence.

Many shop teachers carry individual liability insurance policies, but it is next to impossible to get an accurate count or even an estimate of the number of these individual policies. The choice of an insurance company is left to the discretion of the individual teacher, but it is recommended that these policies be examined most carefully to be certain that the policy provides the protection needed.

Another form of individual liability insurance which has been gaining acceptance in recent years involves a "business pursuits" endorsement, or rider, which can be added to an individual homeowner's package policy. This homeowner's policy in itself would insure for the normal liability necessary in a policy of this type and a personal liability endorsement for business pursuits would be attached to the original. The basic prerequisite here is that the individual involved be a homeowner and have a package policy in effect.

Insurance companies have identified the areas of teaching in which the likelihood of accidental injury is more prevalent and have classified them accordingly. Premiums for liability policies for teachers are also scaled according to this classification. The nature of the subject matter taught and the relative hazardous aspects of the subject matter seem to be the determining factor in the classification of premium groups. Premium group "C," for example, includes those teachers involved in the teaching of athletics, subjects involving laboratory work, manual training (industrial-education teachers), physical training, and swimming. Premium group "D" would include all those teachers not otherwise classified. In both premium groups "C" and "D," liability coverage is complete for claims resulting from pupil injury, with the exception that both exclude liability for corporal punishment.

The premium rates for a "business pursuits" rider on a homeowner's package policy vary with the locale and the situation. Samples indicate, however, that coverage for a three-year period under premium group "C," which includes shop teachers, would be more than twice that for teachers classified under premium group "D."

It might be well to state at this time that it is possible for teachers to insure against liability resulting from corporal punishment of pupils under the business pursuits endorsement. It would be contained under premium group "E," with fees for this protection being additional to the premium paid under premium group "C" or "D."

Self-Insurance

The cost involved when a school district carries liability insurance often appears to be excessive in terms of loss expectancy. In place of this, school districts in large cities might well consider building up their own sinking funds and acting as "self-insurers."

Self-insurance is, in reality, a method whereby reserve funds are accumulated to meet certain contingencies. They may be activated by one or the other of two acceptable programs. One program would allow the school district to assume the loss when it occurs without making prior financial arrangements to provide for the loss. The other alternative would be to establish and build up a reserve fund to meet any loss that might occur. It would appear logical that only the larger school districts could benefit from either of these programs, because a smaller school district would not be able to sustain it financially.

California is one of the states where it is possible for a school district to act as self-insurer. The authorization for this is contained in the California Education Code(*12*), Section 1029.1, and is worded as follows:

> In districts situated within or partly within cities having a population of more than 50,000 any board of education may provide from its own funds for the purpose of covering the liabilty of the district, its officers, agents, and employees, in lieu of carrying insurance in insurance companies as provided in Section 1029. Nothing contained herein shall be construed as prohibiting the board of education of the district from providing protection against such liability partly by means of its own funds and partly by means of insurance written by insurance companies as provided in Section 1029.

(*12*) *Education Code of California,* Printing Division, State of California, Sacramento 1953.

It is assumed that school districts have the power to self-insure unless specifically prohibited by statute. A school district entering into a self-insurance program would do well to complete the transition over a 3- to 5-year period. Sufficient insurance should be maintained during the transition period to provide for any contingency. At that point in time when a reserve has been established, the school district could operate on a totally self-insured basis.

Education Agencies

Organized education agencies or associations in many states stand ready to provide assistance to a public school teacher who has become involved in a liability action resulting from a school accident. This assistance is not forced on an individual, it is available on request. Some education associations at the state level, while readily providing legal assistance, prefer to remain out of the limelight. This is particularly true in those states which do not provide a group liability policy and which are generally referred to as "common-law states."

State education associations provide assistance for teachers more often than other agencies. However, other agencies which have been known to provide assistance include the National Education Association, local education associations, state vocational associations, local and state boards of education, and, in a small number of situations, the state industrial commission. The National Education Association provides consulting services to local associations. Help is available from the Office of the Assistant Executive Secretary for Field Operations, the consultant for local associations, the Research Division, and some of the standing committees. The National Education Association offers investigation, financial aid, and legal-advisory aid, on request, to individual teacher members when the need arises.

A small number of states have made other provisions to protect their teachers and absorb some of the headaches that may arise as a result of a liability suit. In Pennsylvania, each school district has complete autonomy, therefore the state has no jurisdiction in matters of this type.

In Alabama, a person who is employed by an agency of the state and is injured in the performance of his duties may apply to the State Board of Adjustments for payments. Under certain limited circumstances, parents of injured school children may make application to their board of education and receive limited payments.

In the District of Columbia, cases involving legal action are referred to the corporation counsel, which is the legal authority for the District of

Columbia. In addition, injuries to any employee of the District or the federal government incurred on the job will be treated by the United States Public Health Service if the employee so desires.

Summary

Although the courts have been most liberal with public school teachers in their decisions regarding liability and negligence, it must be understood that teachers are still subject to suit resulting from pupil injuries sustained in school accidents and should have some method of assistance or protection to alleviate any financial damages that may be assessed. Two partial answers to the problem of teacher liability are legislation and insurance.

Legislation of benefit to school teachers has been passed in several states. Foremost are the "save-harmless" statutes, which have been enacted in at least five states, and the abrogation or modification of the principle of common-law immunity, which has been enacted in several other states. These statutes allow the school district to assume various degrees of responsibility in regard to teacher liability.

Educators are, have been, and should always be concerned about the safety and well-being of the students entrusted to their care. Since the passage of the William-Steiger Occupational Safety and Health Act of 1970 (OSHA), however, more interest has been focused on potential health hazards in school shops and laboratories. Vocational, technical, and industrial arts teachers have a responsibility to translate the various elements of OSHA into education and training because of their specialized knowledge, thereby allowing young men and women to work safely and successfully in today's technological society.

Although the regulations of the Occupational Safety and Health Act do not now apply to public school systems and state institutions of higher learning, such minimum standards may well be considered as reasonable and proper. Procedures under the Act have not been sufficiently developed to permit an exact assessment of the effect on educational systems and institutions. Until further judicial interpretation and/or state implementation of the Act is made, these questions must remain unanswered. In the meantime, violation of the standards may subject individuals to liability in tort claims where no immunity exists. It then appears appropriate for school administrators, supervisors, and teachers to familiarize themselves with the various provisions as contained in OSHA and other state or municipal regulations.

Safety and OSHA are not synonymous. Safety is a direct application of a set of principles, procedures, and regulations. OSHA provides for a comprehensive program to insure a safer and more healthful work environment. Health concerns are an aspect of indirect student protection. Through OSHA, health concerns have attained parity with safety. A safe and healthful work place should be the rule rather than the exception. This should be the continuing and ultimate goal. In addition, teachers should adopt the missionary approach toward attainment of a change of attitude on behalf of fellow educators as well as students.

Teachers in some states, through their state organizations, have requested legislation to relieve the pressure of personal liability. Several state education associations have attempted to get favorable legislation passed and others have committees at work.

Group liability insurance has been instituted in approximately 47 states. Normally, it is sponsored by the state education association. Personal or individual liability insurance policies are available in all states at the discretion of the individual teachers.

Organized education associations, local, state, and national, provide assistance in many instances for teachers who have been sued as a result of alleged negligence. This assistance is available on request and is part of the service provided by these groups.

The question has been raised as to whether or not teacher immunity from court costs, attorney fees, and the damages evolving from accidents to pupils under their supervision might result in increased teacher negligence, carelessness, or complacency. It has been found, to the contrary, that the protection itself does not generally contribute to carelessness on the part of the individual, but affords an opportunity to develop more poised, happy, successful, and useful teachers. Regardless of the protection against financial loss a teacher may enjoy, there is always the moral obligation for making the learning process safe and for avoiding injury to pupils.

Review Questions

1. How do the statutes of various states differ in regard to teacher and school district liability? What is the current situation in your own state?
2. By what means can the common-law rule of governmental immunity as applied to school districts be revoked?
3. What are some of the significant facts of "save-harmless" laws as applied to education?

4. What is the difference between permissive and mandatory "save-harmless" laws?
5. Is it possible under existing laws to fully relieve public school teachers from liability of negligence for their acts while engaged in teaching?
6. Who is responsible for the administration and enforcement of the Occupational Safety and Health Act of 1970?
7. How are public school systems and state institutions of higher learning affected by the provisions of OSHA?
8. How complete is the insuring agreement under a group liability policy?
9. May school districts in your state provide public school teachers with insurance protection out of public funds?
10. What three alternatives are possible with respect to a school carrying liability insurance?
11. How might the statutes of limitations benefit a school district or an individual teacher? Are they in effect in your state?
12. In what ways can "safe-place" statutes affect public school teachers and school-shop conditions?
13. What assistance might a teacher who is involved in a liability suit expect from the National Education Association? From the state education association? From a local education association?
14. Is it conceivable that a teacher might tend to rely too heavily on protective legislation or insurance and become careless in his teaching habits?
15. In your opinion, how can a teacher best safeguard himself from litigation and possible payment of damages?

CHAPTER 5

Safety: An Instrument in Preventing Liability

LEGISLATION has been provided in some states and in most states insurance is available to teachers to help alleviate any financial loss that may be assessed following a school-related pupil injury. These two elements, however, are not in themselves sufficient to prevent a teacher from being adjudged liable. Accidents cannot be legislated against, nor can an insurance policy prevent an injury. It is the responsibility of the teacher as an individual to take adequate precautions in order to remain free from liability, insofar as it is legally possible. To receive benefit from the means available, the teacher must fulfill certain requirements of conduct. Conditions of a practical nature must be properly controlled by the teacher to avoid being held liable for the injury of pupils in the school shop.

Court cases are resolved only after a thorough review of the actions of the teacher involved. An important piece of the teacher's armor, or protection from liability, is an adequate accident prevention and safety program. This program should include factors such as teaching for the development of safety attitudes, proper safety instructions, the enforcement of safety practices, the provision of a safe working environment, and the use of proper procedures should an accident occur.

Shop teachers have a particularly challenging job. In addition to working with tools, machines, and materials which contain a degree of potential hazard, they may encounter recalcitrant pupils who have a tendency to be reckless and irresponsible. Self-assertive students, not particularly interested in school work, pose a singular problem. Pupils of all classifications may rebel at certain restrictions if they are not presented in a meaningful manner. The entire question of liability depends on whether or not proof of negligence can be established, so an evaluation of the specific conditions which control the actions of the pupils in a shop class is in order. These conditions are physical and human in nature and must be properly controlled by the teacher.

The Concept of Safety

People who are familiar with the public school system of education recognize the potential for pupil accidents in schools. Concern for the immediate welfare of pupils is expected of teachers. This is essential because pupils themselves do not always use the best judgment, often lacking the experience and maturity necessary to make competent decisions. Positive action by teachers is necessary.

A shop teacher is duly responsible for the exercise of safe practices in his own classroom and accepts the protection of pupils from accidental injury as one of his major responsibilities. A mature, well-trained, safety-conscious teacher is essential. Safety consists of more than just dispensing information or developing a set of rules and regulations. Effective instruction involves teaching pupils the right form of behavior in addition to motivating them in the development of acceptable operational skills. These skills can become safety habits. A teacher's disregard of violations of safety regulations could result in a charge of negligence against him. Incidentally, when making reference to safety regulations in the school shop, it is psychologically better to refer to them as safety "practices" rather than "rules."

If a teacher could be so well informed as to be able to enforce a set of perfect safety practices, he could be freed from responsibility for negligent acts and the resultant liability. However, there is no magic formula available and no clear-cut rules that will guarantee complete freedom from liability.

The teacher of shop subjects will do well to use a great deal of forethought to avoid, insofar as possible, all types of accidents in the school shop. Reasonable precautions are required for every shop teacher. Although a teacher usually acts with due care, he must be prepared to prove beyond a doubt, in case of an injury to a pupil, that his actions did not constitute the proximate cause of the accident.

Moral responsibility is as important as legal responsibility, with the two being very closely related. Shop teachers should act honestly and in good faith within their jurisdiction. This jurisdiction and responsibility for the welfare of the pupils is well defined in the laws of some states. An example of this is in the *Laws Relating to the Minnesota Public School System*(*1*). These laws state in part that:

> Every person having the care or custody of a minor who shall
> 1. Willfully cause or permit his life to be endangered, his health to be injured, or his morals to become depraved; or
> 2. Willfully cause or permit such minor to be placed in a situation or to engage in an occupation, which will be likely to endanger his life, injure his health, or impair his morals
>
> . . . shall be guilty of a gross misdemeanor.

As more pupils take shop courses and for extended periods, the shop teacher's responsibility will increase. Administrators should be cognizant of this fact when assigning pupils to a shop class. The number of pupils assigned to a shop class should be in keeping with the available facilities and the human limitations of the individual instructor.

Accidents in the school shop are an economic as well as a humanitarian problem. Litigation resulting from school accidents can prove to be costly in terms of legal fees even though the shop teacher or the school district may be exonerated.

Teachers and administrators need to take every precautionary measure possible to reduce the chances of an accident occurring. Anything that might be done to protect teachers from damages through insurance or legislation does not minimize the need for and importance of a good safety program, excuse poor teaching practices, or condone carelessness in the upkeep of the equipment in the school shop.

The following recommendations are made to assist the teacher in remaining judgment free. In addition to the inspection of facilities at regular intervals, it is recommended that quality equipment be purchased from reliable firms and installed by competent persons. All regular school activities should be supervised by qualified teachers. Provisions should also be made for the proper care of a pupil injured in class.

Causes of School-Shop Accidents

In identifying causes of accidents in the school shop, three components stand out as significant: (1) unsafe conditions, which involve mechanical or physical facilities; (2) unsafe practices, which are violations of procedures commonly accepted as safe; and (3) unsafe personal factors which are mental or physical in nature. These three elements are usually associated with an accidental injury and are often interrelated. They can, and

---

(*1*) Minnesota Department of Education, *Laws Relating to the Minnesota Public School System,* St. Paul, Minnesota. 1953, p. 263.

sometimes do, occur in sequence to produce a personal injury. Preceding the injury there is an occurrence; preceding the occurrence there is usually an unsafe act or an unsafe physical or mechanical condition, or both. In the back of these lie the possible reasons for the unsafe act or unsafe condition. The basic concept in prevention is to discover the causative factors, remove them, and thus attempt to avoid future accidents and injuries of a similar nature.

Mechanical failure or malfunction of a machine in a school shop is unusual if proper maintenance is enforced. The condition of a machine, however, was the prominent factor in the court finding for the plaintiff in *Bowman* v. *Union High School District #1, Kitsap County(2)*. The case involved a charge of negligence on the part of the teacher for which the school district was held liable. Action was brought by the plaintiff following the loss of three fingers while operating a jointer in the school shop. It was alleged that the dullness of the jointer blades was the contributing cause of injury to the pupil. Negligence was based on the failure of the teacher to maintain the jointer in proper operating condition and, further, for allowing the machine to be used without a guard in place.

Personal factors often contribute to unsafe acts. These include indifference caused by improper attitudes, lack of knowledge or skills required to perform an operation, and physical defects. It is assumed that the majority of pupils enrolled in shop classes are relatively free from physical defects which would be detrimental to working safely. If a pupil has a serious physical defect it is recommended that participation be limited to those activities permitted by the disability and that supervision by the teacher be more intense than usual.

Pupils with disabilities pose problems in the school shop which are a little out of the ordinary. Paramount among these are those pupils with defective eyesight, those pupils subject to spastic attacks, and those with other physical malfunctions or mental deficiencies that might hinder the pupil from caring for his own welfare. It is the distinct responsibility of the principal and/or school nurse to make certain that shop teachers are made aware of these pupils. It can be extremely dangerous to have pupils with disabilities working on power equipment and grossly unfair to the teacher if he has not been forewarned about the disability. School counselors, parents, and the family physician play an important role in the satisfactory solution to this problem.

Conditions which were accepted as safe a few years ago are no longer safe

---

(2) *Bowman* v. *Union High School District No. 1,* Kitsap County, 22 P.2d 991. Washington 1933.

in our modern age of science and technology. Thorough basic information is an absolute necessity—partial information merely creates an unwarranted sense of security and may serve to blunt an individual's alertness to danger. The danger enters when a pupil who possesses insufficient skill attempts to perform a task beyond his ability.

Danger is not always visible in some school shops, so it poses unique problems of its own. This is true in electrical or electronics shops where safe practices must be based on an understanding of basic electrical principles and theories. The responsibility of the teacher is greater in these areas because the pupil may not be aware of the obscure technical intricacies of the activity, equipment, or procedures.

The best accident is the one that never occurs. We stand in awe of the progress that has been made in industry to render the manufacturing process safe for the workers, but then realize with chagrin that not enough has been accomplished in the schools. Violations of safe work practices are still quite evident. Hazards are ignored and emergency equipment is inadequate. Housekeeping habits are poor. These facts lead one to believe that not all shop teachers are aware of their precarious position in relation to liability for pupil injuries.

Perhaps one of the more discouraging aspects of accident prevention in the school shop is the failure of individuals to take the necessary precautions to avoid what might be termed a preventable accident. This can be the result of thoughtlessness on the part of the injured pupil, another pupil, or the teacher, based on a lack of sufficient knowledge of, or interest in, the hazards involved.

Development of Safety Attitudes

A positive attitude toward skill development is a prerequisite to the safety of an individual. The teacher is responsible for promoting desirable attitudes that assist pupils in developing a proper respect for safety regulations.

Mechanical aids and devices have been developed and attached to machines in the school shop to protect the pupils from the hazards created by the normal operation of the machines. Success in the utilization of these aids depends on the development of desirable attitudes and proper skills. There is a high correlation between faulty attitudes and lack of knowledge. Athough it may not always be possible to isolate a particular faulty attitude, every possibility should be considered in an honest attempt to identify those traits that tend to increase the vulnerability of pupils to accidents. Efforts can then be directed toward helping the pupils recognize a dangerous situation when it occurs and take the proper precautions.

Human failure is probably the leading cause of accidents. Individuals do not always accept this premise, as each feels he is endowed with a degree of immunity from accidents. This is in itself a dangerous attitude and must be corrected. Many accidents occur in the school shop as a result of a lack of knowledge, a lack of alertness, or preoccupation with other matters. Contributing factors in accidents are anxiety and emotional instability, which cause the pupil to deviate from normal behavior.

Attitudes should be developed that will encourage pupils to work safely in the school shop. Attitudes of personal responsibility should be nurtured throughout every shop course. The pupil can be helped materially by creating an awareness of the seriousness of a situation which may develop when his alertness is reduced or when he is careless.

A Safety Program

The primary purpose of safety instruction is to insure safety and prevent injury to the pupils. A secondary purpose is to prevent or reduce the possibility of legal involvement. Shop teachers have been held personally liable for injuries to pupils who have been permitted to use power machines without first receiving the necessary instructions. A course of study which includes adequate safety instruction is essential. In case of a suit, the teacher's position is stronger if he can prove the pupil has received safety instructions.

In *Kiser* v. *Snyder*(3) evidence presented convinced the court that the plaintiff had been adequately warned of the diverse capabilities of the metal shearing machine. The court, in finding for the defendant, held that the plaintiff had received instruction through a series of demonstrations presented by the teacher.

The effectiveness of safety instruction in the school shop depends to a large extent on the interest of the teacher in making it pertinent and alive. It is also conditioned by the training and ability of the teacher and his familiarity with safety factors. Printed rules, safety slogans, and other visual aids on safety have value, but they can be rendered useless by improper actions or example of the teacher. He must thoroughly and properly demonstrate an operation on the machine and then closely supervise the pupils while they perform the operation. Subsequently, when the teacher himself is operating a machine, he must follow recommended

---

(3) *Kiser* v. *Snyder*, 194 S.E.2d 638. North Carolina 1973. And 205 S.E.2d 619. North Carolina 1974.

procedures and not use shortcuts which may be dangerous.

Only when pupils fully understand the operation and functions of tools and machines in the school shop are they able to protect themselves from potential danger. Many of the safety principles and applications that govern the work in the school shop may also be applied to out-of-school situations. Safety in the school shop has definite carry-over value.

Teaching Shop Safety

The safety lecture, in combination with other methods, forms the nucleus of safety instruction in the school shop. To be effective, it should involve chalkboard presentations, other visual aids, and demonstrations. It should also provide discussion opportunities, depending on the age and maturity level of the group. This material can be supplemented by bulletin boards, posters, safety films, and safety slogans. The ultimate aim is to develop within the pupils the attitude, ability, and desire to perform all the activities in the school shop in a safe manner.

Safety instruction should not be limited to a specified unit but should be stressed throughout the entire course. A continuous application of safety instruction was a deciding factor in *Perumeau* v. *Willis*(4). In this case the plaintiff charged the teacher with negligence when he was injured as a result of an accident in the school auto shop. In granting a verdict in favor of the teacher, the court ruled that safety rules were repeated often and that the pupil was the negligent party and not the teacher.

Safety Tests

Safety tests are measuring devices designed to evaluate how well the pupils have assimilated the information, habits, skills, and attitudes essential to their own safety and well-being. This method of teaching safety in the school shop can be classified into two basic types: written safety tests and manipulative, or performance, safety tests. Both can provide a factual record that safety instruction has been given. Both can be instrumental in clearing a teacher of negligence in case of an accident. It is recommended that the results of safety tests be kept on file, complete with the score and date.

In the event of a recordable accident to the pupil, the pupil's written safety test should be withdrawn from the teacher's file and placed in the file of the supervisor or principal, or forwarded to the insurance or legal section of the school administration. It should be kept there until the pupil reaches legal age and thereby forfeits the right to bring suit, or until

(4) *Perumeau* v. *Willis*, 67 P.2d 96. California 1937.

it is needed as evidence in a court trial. Written safety tests of those pupils who have not experienced a recordable accident should be retained for two or three semesters and then destroyed.

Details concerning the administration of a safety test figured prominently in the court finding for the defendant school district in *Miles* v. *School District #138 of Cheyenne County*(5). After sustaining the loss of two fingers, a 17-year-old female student brought suit against the school district alleging negligence in the conduct of a school shop class. The injury occurred when the student attempted to remove a piece of wood from the jointer while making a bevel cut. The machine guard was in place at the time of the accident. It was brought out during the proceedings that the student was in the second year of enrollment in the school shop class and was thoroughly familiar with the operation of the jointer.

In its findings, the court ruled that the student's negligence in placing her left hand in the rotating blades of the jointer was the sole proximate cause of the injury. The records also confirmed that a safety test was required and had been administered as a part of class procedure. The court argued that the teacher's technique of allowing students who failed the safety examination to submit for approval the correct answers to the questions missed was reasonable. This was in lieu of retaking the entire safety examination.

Even though safety tests give a degree of legal protection to a teacher should an accident materialize, this is not their most important function. The tests themselves should serve as an aid in the instructional process and benefit the pupils by facilitating a better understanding of shop operations.

The degree of achievement necessary to constitute a passing grade must be predetermined and specifically adhered to for both the written and the manipulative-type safety test. Levels of proficiency, standards of achievement, and methods of recordkeeping must be well defined.

A teacher must usually look to his own ingenuity to devise suitable instruments for measuring safety proficiency. To be valid, a safety test must be positive in nature, free from ambiguity, and must present real situations to the pupils. Although objective tests are preferred over subjective tests, the type of test will normally be determined by the nature of the information desired, by the age and maturity level of the group to be tested, and by the purpose which it is to serve. It must also be designed to permit precise scoring.

---

(5) *Miles* v. *School District #138 of Cheyenne County*, 281 N.W. 2d 396,. Nebraska 1979.

Safety tests are not a cure-all for the problems involved in accident prevention, nor are they infallible. They are not intended as a substitute for pertinent information that should be dispensed by lecture, demonstrations, or other safety education techniques. Safety tests can serve as an accident prevention device, but individual teachers must use discretion and not place too much faith in them. There is always a chance for error in interpreting the meaning implied by a question, or in interpreting an answer given in an objective test. A great deal of the success of the instrument depends on the ability of the individual administering it. Failure to pass a safety test does not in itself indicate that the person will have an accident any more than passing the test will make a pupil immune to accidents. Basically, passing the test means that the pupil reasonably understands the operation and can use the equipment and machines safely.

Enforcement of Safe Practices

One of the primary purposes of safety education is to discipline pupils so as to enable them to work and live safely in the world. The safety of the pupils in school activities is the joint responsibility of teachers and the administration. Competent leadership and supervision must be provided for all the pupils at all times. The ultimate success of any accident prevention effort is dependent on the efficiency with which the program is administered.

Accidents can be prevented by human alertness. This can best be achieved by careful attention to the focal points of trouble. Shop teachers have the responsibility of including accident prevention in their instruction and being certain that all safety rules are enforced. It is their duty to carry out immediately any recommendations of their supervisors which are intended to improve working conditions. Shop teachers must also be prepared to make recommendations to supervisors to improve safety conditions when this seems desirable.

In 1977, the State of New Jersey took a giant step forward when it approved a system for the implementation of a vocational education safety standards program. This is perhaps the most complete program on record and recognizes the importance of a state system in supporting the safety movement in public education. Rules and regulations were prescribed and approved by the State Board of Education. These rules were designed to provide safety standards that would govern the use of tools, machines, equipment, and protective devices in vocational education programs and courses. Section 6:53-2.2 of Subchapter 2 and Chapter 53 of the New Jersey State Education Law clearly mandates the development of a safety program. All boards of education operating courses and/or programs in vocational education are required to organize, adopt, and implement a safety education program. The safety education program shall contain as a minimum the following sections:

1. Objectives of the safety education program.
2. A statement of general policies for the safe operation of vocational courses.
3. Specific statements of practices and precautions required for safe operations in each separate course.
4. A plan for periodic inspection and maintenance of facilities, tools, machines, equipment, and personal protective devices.
5. A plan for the identification and elimination of potential hazards.
6. Emergency procedures to be followed in the event of an accident involving a student, teacher, or any other individual.
7. Methods to be used to provide safety education to students.
8. Methods to be used to assess a student's knowledge of safe practices and procedures.

Supervision

Shop teachers' contracts to teach normally provide that they shall have charge of a stated grade, teach a particular subject or serve in a designated department, and abide by the rules and regulations handed down by the school district. In the great majority of contracts there is no specific provision spelling out the supervisory duties of the teacher. A legal question then arises as to the extent of duty implied under this contract and what criterion is to be used in determining what constitutes adequate supervision. In view of the uncertainty of the law in determining just what supervision is necessary, it behooves the teacher to use utmost care. Any hazard to the safety of the pupils that can be guarded against by appropriate supervision then becomes the duty of the teacher.

The courts have been most severe in their criticism of school administrations which require pupils to perform experiments or to operate certain machines that subject them to dangers without requiring that the strictest supervision be exercised over them. This exacting supervision is essential if the school district is to escape liability. Indiana statutes provide that minor children are not permitted to operate certain power tools unless they are participating in a supervised industrial arts or vocational education class that uses properly guarded equipment.

Some teachers allow only a few of the more mature pupils to operate complex machinery. The teacher is expected to perform these operations for the other pupils. However, it is common knowledge that the safe use of tools and machines cannot be taught by having pupils avoid situations where there is a remote possibility of being injured. It is the responsibility of the teacher to recognize hazardous situations and help pupils avoid danger. In a large class there is need for an exceptional degree of alertness. Emphasis on safe conduct and safe work habits becomes essential.

A teacher who leaves a class unsupervised may be considered negligent if an injury to a pupil results from lack of supervision. Court decisions notwithstanding, leaving a classroom while the class is in session is fraught with legal hazards should a student injury occur. Teachers could expect that absence from assigned duties in a classroom would increase the tendency for horseplay and chance taking. A teacher's primary responsibility is to the students. If teachers are expected to assume secondary responsibilities such as hall or cafeteria supervision, they are free to participate providing—and only providing—students in the classroom have been adequately cared for. A printed list of rules of conduct does not constitute supervision or substitute for a teacher. If an injury occurs while a teacher is absent from the classroom, it appears immaterial whether the exact injury and proximate cause thereof was foreseen. The rule invoked in assessing negligence based on an allegation of failure to supervise is a clearly recognized principle in tort law—"Against the probability and gravity of risk of harm must be balanced the utility of the conduct." If a shop teacher is called on to leave the shop even momentarily while the class is in session, it is recommended that power machines be shut off and safely locked.

Continuous and untiring safe-practice supervision is necessary in the school shop. This is true regardless of the degree of skill attained by the pupils because they may become careless, overconfident of their ability, or may short cut the safety process. They may take chances by circumventing protective devices and ignoring safety rules. The teacher has a legal responsibility to check conduct of this type, as evidenced in the case of *Dutcher* v. *City of Santa Rosa High School District*(6) which resulted from the death of one pupil and major injuries to another. The verdict was in favor of the plaintiff, with the court ruling that the teacher had failed to enforce rules and regulations of safety in the auto shop. The court also stated that the teacher had failed to supervise pupils who did not appreciate the danger of an explosion and who were using an acetylene torch near a gasoline tank.

---

(6) *Dutcher* v. *City of Santa Rosa High School District*, 290 P.2d 316. California 1957.

A judgment similar to this was handed down in *Govel* v. *Board of Education of City of Albany*(7). The accident occurred when a pupil, other than the plaintiff, was testing a gun which had been brought in for repairs. The gun misfired, injuring the plaintiff. The shop teacher was held negligent and the school district held liable for not adequately supervising the work and warning the pupils who were within range of the danger. These two cases are further proof that the law is cognizant of the fact that children are not expected to possess the same degree of foresight, prudence, and knowledge as adults and that children may not be judged according to the same standard of care as adults.

Failure to warn of dangers caused a teacher to be declared negligent and the school district liable in *Calandri* v. *Ione Unified School District of Amador County*(8). Although the agent, a scale model of a Revolutionary-War-type cannon, was constructed in class, the accident occurred at home. The court ruled that the teacher's evident failure to warn of the danger involved in loading and firing a cannon constituted the proximate cause of the resultant injuries. Further details of this case are contained in Chapter 3.

A well established and supervised safety program can be an asset to a shop teacher, as was true in *Klenzendorf* v. *Shasta Union High School District*(9). The plaintiff filed suit as a result of the loss of fingers while working on the jointer in the wood shop. The court, in finding for the defendants, ruled the district and the teacher not liable for the injury to the pupil because the pupil had been given thorough instruction in the safe operation of the equipment, and appropriate signs were posted.

A questionable practice is the assignment of an uncooperative pupil to a responsible safety position in an attempt to alleviate a discipline problem and stimulate interest in school work. This can prove to be dangerous and may lead to legal implications for the teacher should an accident result.

It should also be noted that the practice of sending pupils on errands outside of the school building is charged with danger. Under no circumstances can this be regarded as a part of the school program. Pupils are not messengers and cannot be regarded as such by teachers even though

---

(7) *Govel* v. *Board of Education of City of Albany,* 60 N.E.2d 133. New York 1944.

(8) *Calandri* v. *Ione Unified School District of Amador County,* 33 Cal. Rptr. 333. California 1963.

(9) *Klenzendorf* v. *Shasta Union High School District,* 40 P.2d 878. California 1935.

a school function is involved in connection with the errand.

The amount of care, or absence thereof, demonstrated by a person's action is usually a question for the jury. No set of standards or rules can be used to insure behavior on the part of the teacher that will make him immune from liability, nor can any law protect a man from his own mistakes. The teacher must assist the pupils in the realization that the school district has attempted to provide a safe environment and that they are expected to contribute their efforts toward safe work. Compliance by coercion is not the recommended procedure, but it may become necessary in extreme cases. The shop teacher who makes a conscientious attempt to foresee possible risks and who guards against the potential dangers will best serve his own interests as well as those of his pupils.

Machine Guarding

Machine guarding in school shops involves a dual responsibilty, shared by the school district and the individual teacher. It is the duty of the school district to provide adequate guards on all machines, and the duty of the teacher to see that they are used. Most machines utilized in the school shop come equipped with safety guards. The development of safety apparatus through scientific research has kept pace with new equipment. The problem is that there are perhaps more protective devices than there are persons willing to use them. Many accidents occur because people refuse to, or fail to, take the necessary precautions to protect themselves. The courts have affirmed the responsibility of teachers in determining the type of power tools to be purchased and the safety features to be included thereon. The school district has an implied obligation to properly install and maintain the equipment.

If pupils are permitted to use unguarded machines in the school shop, the teacher is without question guilty of negligence should an accident occur. Whenever possible, the guard should be an integral part of the machine and be designed primarily for the protection of the operator and observers. Safe design takes into account the exposure of personnel to accident, but it should never hamper operation or obstruct vision. Machine guards should be substantial, simple in construction, reliable, easy to operate and maintain, and firmly installed.

The theory of machine guarding involves four basic principles. The first, or primary, principle is that safety devices shall function in such a manner that physical contact between the operator and moving parts of the machine becomes virtually impossible. When it is not possible or practical to fulfill this requirement, mechanical guards of one type or another are added.

The second principle is that any safety device on a machine shall operate in such a manner as to prevent or minimize the possibility of injury from an accident. This principle is based on the premise that by the use of proper guards injury can be prevented or the incident rate can be appreciably reduced. The guard shall be of such a nature that it does not offer a hazard in itself.

The third principle of machine guarding is that safety factors incorporated in a machine shall function properly. Circuit breakers, cutout switches, and motor overloads are examples of this principle.

The fourth principle of machine guarding involves control. It requires the machine to be so designed and equipped that it operates only in accordance with the wishes of the operator. Control buttons or switches must be properly located and designed to prevent inadvertent action. The starting control should be recessed to prevent accidental activation. Conversely, stop controls must be prominently located for easy activation in case of an emergency. Machines and equipment whose operation requires the presence of an operator shall not be left unattended while in operation.

Improperly guarded machines in the school shop have figured prominently in many court cases involving shop teachers and school districts. In several cases*(10)*, it appears that only the application of the principle of governmental immunity saved the school district from damage claims. In other words, it was proved in court that the machines in question were not properly guarded, although damages were denied the plaintiff. It is evident that the teacher was a prominent party in this deficiency because injuries grew out of the failure of the teacher to require the pupil to use the safeguards provided by the board of education.

Not all cases involving inadequate machine guarding in the school shop have been decided in favor of the school district and the teacher*(11)*.

---

(10) Conrad v. *Board of Education of Ridgeville Township,* 163 N.E.567, Ohio 1928; *Johnson* v. *Board of Education of City of Hudson,* 206 N.Y.S. 610, New York 1924; *Kirchoff* v. *City of Janesville,* 38 N.W.2d 698, Wisconsin 1949; *Krutili* v. *Board of Education of Butler District,* 129 S.E. 486, West Virginia 1925; *Sullivan* v. *School District No. 1 of City of Tomah,* 191 N.W. 1020, Wisconsin 1923; *Nabell* v. *City of Atlanta,* 126 S.E. 905, Georgia 1925; *Niedfeldt* v. *Joint School District No. 1 of City of Viroqua,* 127 N.W.2d 800, Wisconsin 1964; *Crabbe* v. *County School Board of Northumberland County,* 164 S.E.2d 639, Virginia 1968.

(11) Scott County School District #1 v. *Asher,* 312 N.E.2d 131, Indiana 1974; *South Ripley Community School Corporation* v. *Peters and Powermatic-Houdaille,* 396 N.E.2d 144, Indiana 1979.

In *Ahern* v. *Livermore Union High School*(*12*), judgment was returned in favor of the plaintiff and against the school district. Action was brought after a pupil lost two fingers when his hand came into contact with a power-saw blade while he was cutting a groove in a piece of scrap lumber. Evidence brought out in court indicated that the pupils in the class were not instructed as to the necessity of using a guard when operating the saw.

The teacher's poor example was a contributing factor in the court's decision in favor of the plaintiff in *Ridge* v. *Boulder Creek*(*13*). The plaintiff injured a finger on his right hand while operating a power saw without a guard or a fence in position. Evidence presented in court substantiated the plaintiff's claim that the teacher used the saw without a guard, as did other pupils in the class. The district was, therefore, held liable under the California statute. Other cases of court record bear out the fact that the school district and teachers of shop subjects have a definite responsibility in providing guards for machines and insisting that they be in position and use whenever the machine is in operation(*14*).

Adequate and well functioning guards on the machines in a school shop are visible evidence that this phase of the school's responsibility has been satisfied. However, there is one danger in the emphasis on the use of guards which must be avoided. This danger involves the implication that if a machine is guarded, it provides a degree of freedom for the operator which could lead to careless actions and possible injury.

Adequate mechanical safeguards have succeeded in reducing the number and severity of accidents in industry. Mechanical guards must be in postion and used whenever the machine is in operation if they are to perform the function for which they were designed. This is true in school shops as well, because many of the machines are industrial in nature and function.

Eye Safety

An analysis of accident statistics reveals the alarming fact that serious injuries continue to occur in the nation's schools, resulting in damage to

---

(*12*) *Ahern* v. *Livermore Union High School,* 284 P. 1105. California 1930.

(*13*) *Ridge* v. *Boulder Creek,* 140 P.2d 990. California 1943.

(*14*) *Banks* v. *Seattle School District No. 1,* 80 P.2d 835, Washington 1938; *Herman* v. *Board of Education of Union School District No. 8,* 137 N.E. 24, New York 1925; *Lehmann* v. *Los Angeles City Board of Education,* 316 P.2d 55, California 1957; *Reeder* v. *Board of Education of New York City,* 50 N.E. 2d 236, New York 1943.

the eyes and loss of sight. These injuries occur at a rate that is unacceptable by any standards. The message to teachers should be clear. Teach what some might regard as obvious—the value of protecting and maintaining one of the most valuable of the five senses—unimpaired vision. The major objective to be reached is the total elimination of accidental eye injuries for all of those who participate in educational activities.

Eye safety is one phase of school accident prevention which still seems to be lagging. Educational institutions in general have been slow to accept eye safety as an integral phase of class activity. Many new and modern school plants have well planned shops and laboratories but still lack an eye-protection program. The number of eye injuries in schools demands positive action.

Eye injuries have figured heavily in court cases involving school personnel*(15)*. Various conditions and factors were involved in these cases, but almost without fail, loss of an eye was the result. Unusual circumstances were involved in *Thomas* v. *City of New York(16)*. In finding in favor of the plaintiff, the court uncovered evidence that the plaintiff suffered the loss of an eye when a scriber, which had been inserted and clamped in the chuck of a machine lathe, flew out of its fastening. Equally unusual were the circumstances surrounding the loss of an eye in *Srnka* v. *Joint District No. ((17)*. In this case, the plaintiff suffered the loss of an eye when another pupil poked a steel file through a knothole in a door through which the plaintiff was looking.

Frequently, eye mishaps occur to pupils not directly exposed to obvious hazards. This was true in *Goodman* v. *Pasadena City High School District(18)*. Action resulted from the loss of an eye sustained by a pupil in a machine-shop class while watching, from a distance of about 12 feet, another pupil pound aluminum in a vise. A piece of the aluminum broke off and flew into the pupil's eye, destroying it. In ruling on this case, the court

---

(15) *Lilienthal* v. *San Leandro Unified School District,* 298 P.2d 889, California 1956; *Meade* v. *Oakland High School District of Alameda County,* 298 P. 987, California 1931; *Ohman* v. *Board of Education of New York City,* 90 N.E.2d 474, New York 1949; *Ross* v. *San Francisco Unified School District,* 260 P.2d 663, California 1953; *Campbell* v. *Board of Education,* 389 P.2d 464, Utah 1964; *Butler* v. *District of Columbia,* 417 F.2d 1150, District of Columbia 1969; *Hammond* v. *Scott,* 232 S.E.2d 336, South Carolina 1977.

(16) *Thomas* v. *City of New York,* 35 N.E.2d 617. New York 1941.

(17) *Srnka* v. *Joint District No. 3,* 182 N.W. 325. Wisconsin 1921.

(18) *Goodman* v. *Pasadena City High School District,* 40 P.2d 854. California 1935.

found for the school district, pointing out that there was no proof that any school authority of the district was aware that aluminum would shatter when pounded. The pupils in this class had been instructed to wear safety goggles when striking steel together and while working around a grinding wheel, but it was not deemed necessary to wear goggles at other work in the shop.

A suitable type of eye protection has been developed for every type of eye hazard found in the school shop. One of the surest ways of safeguarding eyes is to institute a 100-percent eye-protection program. This means, in essence, that the teacher, all the pupils, and any visitors are required to wear eye protection at all times the class is in session. Teachers report an increased safety consciousness on the part of the pupils in those schools which have instituted such a program. The advantages of eye protection and eye-protective devices have been recognized by safety experts for more than a quarter of a century. Because of this recognition, industry has effectively reduced ocular damage and loss of sight. It is clear that eye injuries decline sharply when personal protective devices are required. More than 50,000 members of the Wise Owl Club(*19*) can attest personally to this fact. Some of the more progressive industries have required safety eyewear for all employees since as early as 1916.

A successful eye-protection program is dependent on good planning, good protective devices, good safety practices, good maintenance, and good enforcement. To insure program success, school administrators, supervisors, and department chairmen should assume roles similar to those of industrial safety directors. This will get them involved with the total program and provide an excellent opportunity to become more knowledgeable about the condition of tools, equipment, and general physical facilities. Accordingly, they will have occasion to research, plan, and administer safety programs. They will also have a positive hand in the selection and purchase of required personal protective equipment. In the selection of eye-protective devices, competent authorities should be consulted. Representatives of reputable vendors are not only willing, but qualified, to assist schools in planning eye-safety programs and in advising on the selection of approved eye-protective devices. Requiring safety

(*19*) Administered by the National Society for the Prevention of Blindness, Inc., 79 Madison Avenue, New York, NY 10016. Exclusive membership restricted to technical students and industrial workers who have saved one or both eyes by wearing eye and face protective devices meeting requirements of the "American National Standard Practice for Occupational and Educational Eye and Face Protection, Z87.1-1979," or later revisions thereof.

eyewear suppliers to certify on their business letterhead that devices they furnish comply in every respect to the ANSI Z87 standard and will ensure maximum protection in the legal as well as the physical sense. Visitors' eyewear intended for temporary use invariably does not meet ANSI requirements.

It is difficult to determine or even to estimate the actual number of eyes saved by eye-safety programs in the schools. Industry, however, can forcefully point out the importance of eye safety by the substantial decrease in the incidence of eye accidents and injuries. Statistics from one large industrial firm in particular prove the worth of an eye-safety program. Eye injuries decreased so dramatically in a test segment of selected workers that the program was expanded to include all machine-shop personnel. Eventually every employee of the manufacturing division was provided with safety glasses and required to wear them. In the first year this program was in operation, total eye-injury accidents dropped from 320 to 138. Five years later the yearly total was only 39 despite an increase in the number of employees in the manufacturing division. These statistics emphasize the value of 100-percent eye protection for all personnel, whether in industry or the school shop.

Eye-Safety Legislation

The legislative bodies of most states have become actively involved in legislative enactments that either directly or indirectly affect the educational process. Perhaps the most positive action taken to date is the introduction of mandatory school eye-safety legislation.

Late in 1962, a dedicated group of Ohio citizens commenced work on a project that ultimately resulted in the first mandatory school eye-safety law. The driving force behind the effort was legislator Mrs. Clara Weisenborn. The resulting law, House Bill No. 492, was made effective in August 1963 by the Ohio Legislature. The Ohio law was amended in 1972 to include private schools, colleges, and universities.

The Ohio Legislature set a precedent for school eye-safety legislation that has since been emulated by 35 states*(20)*. Interest appeared to have reached a peak in 1965 when 12 states enacted school eye-safety legislation.

In 1970, the District of Columbia City Council passed a regulation to require all students in public and private schools to wear protective eye goggles when engaged in laboratory or shop procedures which might cause damage to the eyes. Two states, Maine and New Mexico, are

---

(20) See Appendix G.

governed by a state-wide school eye-safety directive, mandated by the state department of education.

A model school eye-safety law(*21*), developed under the guidance of James E. O'Neil, former Director of Industrial Services for the National Society for the Prevention of Blindness, has been followed in most instances. Legislative provisions deviate to a degree from state to state, but in essence require that all students, teachers, classroom visitors, and observers wear approved eye-protective devices while participating in certain vocational, industrial arts, and chemical-physical course or laboratories. These devices must be of industrial quality and meet or exceed the standards set by the American National Standards Institute (ANSI). Twenty-nine of the 36 school eye-safety laws now in effect stipulate either Z2.1-1959, Z87.1-1968, or Z87.1-1979 as the minimum standard for eye- and face-protective devices.

Several of the state laws do not appear to cover all eventualities and applications. Although visitors and observers are included in the wording of 31 of these laws, only 19 specifically include provision for private schools and only 20 make mention of colleges and universities. The most common deficiency noted in the laws was the lack of emphasis on enforcement. It could be assumed that enforcement is implied with the passage of the state law, but court interpretations are unpredictable. Enforcement provisions are included in the legislation of only six states: California, Colorado, Iowa, Minnesota, New Jersey, and Pennsylvania, plus the District of Columbia. The Pennsylvania law contains a rather general enforcement provision which places the responsibility on the State Board of Education. It reads: "Enforcement of this act shall be in accordance with standards, rules, and regulations promulgated by the State Board of Education." The New Jersey law varies slightly from the Pennsylvania law in that it places the enforcement responsibilty on the local boards of education in stating, "The board of education of every school district shall require each pupil and teacher in the public schools of the district to wear quality eye-protective devices while attending classes in . . .".

The enforcement provisions in the California and Colorado laws are similar but lack specific authority to penalize for noncompliance. The California law reads: "It shall be the duty of the superintendents, principals, or teachers charged with the supervision of any class in which any such course is conducted to require such eye-protective devices to be worn by students, teachers, and visitors under the circumstances prescribed in Section 12091." The Colorado law is analogous to the Cali-

---

(*21*) See Appendix H.

fornia law in stating, "It shall be the duty of the person charged with the supervision of any such course or activity to require such eye-protective devices to be worn by students, teachers, and visitors under the circumstances prescribed in Section 123-36-2."

Iowa and Minnesota school eye-safety laws contain the most complete enforcement and penalty provisions. The Iowa bill begins: "It shall be the duty of the teacher or other persons supervising the students in said courses to see that the above requirements are complied with." (From here on the Iowa and Minnesota bills are identical.) "Any student failing to comply with such requirements may be temporarily suspended from participation in said course and the registration of a student for such course may be cancelled for willful, flagrant, or repeated failure to observe the above requirements." It is noted that both the Minnesota and Iowa laws specify a penalty for noncompliance on the part of the student. None of the existing laws contain enforcement provisions or penalty clauses for the noncomplying school or teacher.

The Minnesota law was tested in *Scott* v. *Independent School District #709, Duluth(22)*. A seventh-grade student in an industrial arts class suffered permanent damage to his left eye while operating a drill press without wearing eye protection. The student was attempting to drill a hole in a plastic domino when the bit stuck and the drill press shut off. A second student used a pipe wrench to hold the domino in place. As the drill press was turned back on, the drill bit snapped and a tiny piece of the bit lodged in the student's left eye.

Action was brought to recover for the loss of the eye claiming that the school district had, in violation of the state statute, not consistently enforced the rule requiring the use of protective eyewear by students. At the beginning of the school year, an individual pair of safety goggles was assigned to each student. Students were instructed to wear safety goggles, but the regulation was not consistently enforced by the teacher. The court, in ruling in favor of the student and against the school district, held that the school district was negligent for failure to enforce a statute even though some effort had been made to do so.

The school district appealed and the Supreme Court affirmed the decision of the lower court. In doing so, the Supreme Court held that the school district was negligent when it failed to properly supervise and enforce the wearing of safety goggles in an industrial arts class. The student in this situation lost an eye as a result of not wearing the required safety

---

(22) *Scott* v. *Independent School District #709, Duluth,* 256 N.W.2d 485. Minnesota 1977.

equipment. The court decided on an award of $60,000 but declared the student to be contributorily negligent. The actual damages awarded to the student were $50,000. This figure exceeded the insurance coverage and the school district was required to make up the difference.

The authority to purchase and the method of financing eye-protective devices are not clear in all of the laws. In fact, no method of procurement or financing is identified in seven of the laws. Sixteen state laws stipulate that the local board of education *may* provide eye-protective devices while 14 state that the local board of education *shall* provide eye-protective devices.

The development of guidelines by the state board of education is required by the laws of 15 states. Only the Michigan law with an effective date of September 1972 makes direct reference to the need for mandatory sanitation and health procedures.

A 1971 ruling by the Supreme Judicial Court of Massachusetts*(23)* raises the issue as to whether or not an inadequate or incomplete school eye-safety law is better than none at all. The Court found in favor of a chemistry teacher in an action brought by a student who suffered permanent eye damage in a laboratory accident while he was not wearing safety glasses. The charge against the teacher was negligence by reason of misfeasant conduct. The Court found no duty to require the wearing of safety glasses in spite of the beginning statement of the 1964 Massachusetts law which reads: "The school committee of each city or town shall require each pupil and teacher in a public school to wear industrial quality eye-protective devices approved by the Department of Public Safety while attending classes in vocational or industrial-arts shops or laboratories in which caustic or explosive chemicals . . .". One can only speculate as to the basic reasoning of the court, but it appears evident that they did not construe the law as covering activities in the chemistry laboratory. The chemistry laboratory was not specifically mentioned in the wording of the law. The law only refers to "vocational or industrial-arts shops or laboratories . . .". The Massachusetts Court further stated that even assuming that the teacher was bound to require the wearing of safety glasses, he could not be held guilty of misfeasance or mere inaction.

School eye-safety legislation will someday be in effect in all 50 states and the District of Columbia. Provisions and conditions contained in federal laws such as the Occupational Safety and Health Act of 1970 (OSHA) will serve to stimulate school and college accident prevention programs in

---

(23) Desmarais v. *Wachusett Regional School District,* 276 N.E. 2d 691. Massachusetts 1971.

all states, including those without current coverage. Although the stated purpose of OSHA is to assure safe and healthful working conditions for every working man and woman, its implication for educational institutions cannot be disregarded. For those states now considering school eye-safety legislation, certain conditions must be given adequate attention. The following guidelines are recommended to assure a complete and effective piece of legislation:

1. A thorough analysis of existing school eye-safety laws and department of education rulings.
2. Specifically stated technical provisions with the control centered in the state department of education.
3. A mandatory charge of responsibility for implementation and administration at the local school district level.
4. A clear definition of the nature of instructional activities requiring the wearing of eye-protective devices.
5. A specific statement requiring all eye-protective devices to meet or exceed the requirements of the ANSI Z87.1-1979 standard, or later revisions thereof.
6. Involvement of representatives from business, industry, and education in the formulation of accident prevention regulations, policies, and procedures.
7. Inclusion of a clear, concise statement spelling out the prescribed method of procurement and financing of personal protective and other safety devices.
8. Enforcement provisions complete with adequate penalties to be assessed against students, teachers, administrators, and school districts for noncompliance.
9. Require the state department of education in cooperation with the state department of health to prepare guidelines for the development of sanitation and health policies and procedures, referencing guidelines in the ANSI Z87 standard.
10. By definition, include elementary schools, secondary schools, vocational schools, community or junior colleges, colleges, and universities, both public and private.

Care and Maintenance of Physical Facilities

The shop teacher is obligated to exercise due care, with respect to the pupils under his control, in the use of whatever equipment is available. It is the duty of the teacher to provide a safe room for his pupils, even to the extent of guarding against unsafe conditions due to the building itself. Careful scrutiny of the tools and equipment used by the pupils should be a regular habit of the teacher. A safe building, safe equipment, proper guards on machines, and adequate housekeeping practices are all factors which make for a safe and productive working environment. Floors in the working area surrounding all machines shall be provided with effective protection against slipping.

School authorities are responsible for providing school shops with good quality machines and tools, equipped with adequate guards that at least meet the safety standards of the state department of labor and industry. The following example emphasizes the feelings of a court in regard to the provision of safety equipment. Failure to provide safety equipment was held by a New York court as negligence on the part of the school district(*24*). In ruling on this case, the court said, "It seems clear that the legislature did not intend that children in schools should be subjected to danger of serious injury because of lack of equipment which it was requiring employers to furnish to men [in industry]."

The pupil crushed his thumb in an attempt to disentangle his sweater from the wood lathe which he was operating. The plaintiff maintained that the school was negligent when it failed to provide a protective apron. The court ruled for the plaintiff and called attention to section 2510 of the New York Education Law which makes it the duty of the board of education to "furnish equipment as might be necessary for proper and efficient management of education activities under the board's management and control."

It is the duty of the shop teacher to either maintain equipment in safe working order, or to report unsafe circumstances to the proper authority. Failure to anticipate and report hazardous circumstances may place the teacher in a precarious position. The condition of the equipment or tool by which a pupil is injured has bearing on the teacher's liability. Dull or broken tools should be properly reconditioned for use or discarded. It is also possible that precarious placement of equipment and supplies may be the cause of an accident. Adequate space must be provided for each machine and activity. All machines and equipment, with the exception of portable machines and equipment, should be secured in accordance with the procedures recommended by the manufacturer to prevent creeping or moving.

Control over the environmental conditions and physical facilities of the school shop can be made easier by use of a checklist. A well-designed and frequently used checklist provides written evidence that defects or unsafe conditions have been reported to the proper authorities. This type of record should be typed in duplicate with the teacher carefully retaining one

---

(*24*) *Edkins* v. *Board of Education of New York City,* 41 N.E.2d 75. New York 1942.

copy so he can use it as evidence if ever needed. Recommendations from any checklist report must be carried out as soon as practical in order to be effective. This would definitely be to the teacher's advantage should a serious injury occur and a lawsuit result. The checklist can also provide a valuable evaluation of current shop conditions.

First-Aid Procedures

Liability is not limited to acts of negligence preceding or occurring at the time of the initial injury. There have been cases in which teachers have been charged with negligence for their actions, or failures to act, following injurious accidents. Whether or not to administer treatment subsequent to the injury of a pupil constitutes a risk that must be taken with the hope that the court or jury will hold the defendant blameless for what he does or does not do. This is based on prudence. By reason of the relationship of the teacher to the pupil *(in loco parentis)* the teacher is obligated to do the best he can for the pupil in the event of an injury. It is to the teacher's distinct advantage to be trained in at least the rudiments of first aid.

First aid is the immediate, temporary care given the victim of an accident *until* the services of a physician and/or a school nurse can be obtained. In an emergency, a teacher not only has the legal right to administer first aid but would in all probability be considered derelict in his duty if he did not attempt to act for the benefit of the pupils. However, teachers should not attempt treatment beyond first aid under any circumstances. It should be emphasized that teachers are not expected to possess expert medical knowledge.

Expert medical inspection and treatment should be sought immediately for any serious injury sustained by a pupil. It is the duty of the teacher to send the injured pupil to the school nurse or school physician, or to have them come to the scene. If this aid is not available, the parents should be called for instructions. If the parents cannot be reached, the family physician should be called. If an extreme emergency exists and no professional medical service is readily available, first-aid treatment would undoubtedly be upheld in court even though the results of the treatment might be unknowingly harmful.

A knowledge of first aid and quick action by a teacher can often serve the best interests of the school and the pupils. A case in point involves an explosion in the chemistry laboratory of Belmont High School in Los Angeles, California, in which a pupil was seriously injured. Details of this accident indicate complete disregard of established safety principles and instructions by the injured pupil. Suit was not filed in this accident, but it is interesting to note that the two teachers first on the scene following the accident did such a creditable job of administering first aid that they were subsequently honored by a special Red Cross citation.

Teachers should use considerable discretion and only administer that aid sufficient to prevent serious aggravation of the injury. Teachers may be held liable for damages should they attempt treatment beyond their jurisdiction. In one of the few cases of court record involving medical treatment of school pupils(*25*), the teacher was held liable when the court ruled that the situation in question did not constitute an emergency. The plaintiff in this case was said to have had an infected hand which the teacher treated by immersing it in a pan of extremely hot water for a period of 10 minutes. This treatment scalded the hand, aggravated the infection, and resulted in the hospitalization of the pupil. Even though the teacher stood *in loco parentis* to the pupil, there was nothing construed in this relationship that justified the action taken. The defendant did not have medical training, nor was she the school nurse.

In the case of first-aid treatment, the acts must be for the benefit of the injured pupil and bear the sign of good common sense. Teachers have been known to prescribe treatment which is over and beyond their authority. This is a practice which should be discontinued before a serious situation develops. It has been held that school districts in some states have implied authority to provide first aid, but no authority to pay an attending physician other than the school-contracted physician.

Waiver Permission Statements

Parental permission slips or variations of waiver forms were originally intended to relieve the teacher of responsibility in accident cases. When used as a defense mechanism or a device to avoid legal action in the event of an injury, they are often misinterpreted by teachers and administrators as well as by pupils and their parents. Even though a parent gives written consent for a child to participate in activities involving the use of potentially hazardous machines, tools, or materials, this does not absolve the teacher of responsibility for the the safety and welfare of the pupils under his care. In the event of an injury, a teacher is just as liable for negligence as if he had not secured parental consent.

Teachers and school administrators should place limited faith in signed statements from parents, other adults, or from the pupils themselves that

(*25*) *Guerrieri* v. *Tyson,* 24 A.2d 468. Pennsylvania 1942.

seem to relieve teachers or other personnel from legal responsibility. Permission slips are valueless as a release because a parent cannot legally waive the responsibilty of the teacher for his child. In signing a release or waiver form, a parent only waives the right to sue for medical and other expenses resulting from an accident, plus the loss of the child's services. However, the child may still sue.

Teachers of shop subjects are encouraged to continue using parental permission forms, but not as an attempt to release them from their legal responsibility. A parental permission form, properly signed, would indicate that instructions had been given and that the parents had at least given permission for the student to participate. It can serve as a public relations instrument, advising the parents of some of the activities which are a normal part of the class. A variation of the waiver permission form that has been used with some success is the machine permit form in which the parent gives consent for a child to operate certain power machines in a given class. On this form, a parent also has the option of crossing out any machine he does not wish the child to operate.

When a Pupil Is Injured

In the event of a serious injury in the school shop, a predetermined standardized procedure should be followed—standardized, that is, to the extent that there are certain essential things that must be done, but with full realization that each injury-producing accident is a special case. The procedure can be broken down into two distinct phases, primary and secondary.

Primary considerations are those things which must be done immediately following any injury. Secondary considerations would include all other actions to be taken after the confusion has lessened. This is not in any way to be interpreted to mean that secondary considerations are to be postponed, but that there are certain things which of necessity must be done first. Secondary considerations should be completed as soon as practical following an injury.

Primary Considerations

Primary considerations relate directly to the care and welfare of the injured pupil. This is paramount. The degree of care necessary would be determined by the seriousness of the injury. Certain basic steps are recommended in caring for an injured pupil:

1. Attempt to ascertain how seriously the pupil is injured. If there is any doubt, get assistance.

2. If medical assistance is needed, send for aid immediately.
3. Apply only that first aid which is essential and nothing further.
4. Notify immediate supervisor or principal.
5. If pupil is seriously injured, request administrative office to notify the parents and family physician.
6. If pupil has a minor injury but needs the assistance of the school nurse, send injured pupil to nurse's office accompanied by another pupil. Never send an injured pupil alone.
7. If a foreign article enters the eye, immobilize the eye by covering it with a sterile compress and obtain medical assistance immediately. Under no circumstances should a teacher attempt to remove a foreign body from the eye.
8. If an eye has been injured by an acid or an alkali, immediately irrigate with copious amounts of water and obtain medical assistance.
9. Report all injuries, both major and minor, to the school nurse.

Individual school systems will have established procedures which may differ from these listed. They will normally conform to specific state and local regulations governing the care of injured pupils. It is imperative that teachers be aware of these regulations and follow them to the letter. Many times it is just as important for the teacher to know what *not* to do following an accident, as it is to know what action to take.

Secondary Considerations

After the immediate needs of the injured pupil are cared for, the teacher has additional responsibilities which stem directly from an accident. These responsibilities are contained in the area designated as secondary considerations. Recommended steps and procedures would include the following:

1. Stabilize and reassure the other members of the class.
2. Fill out an accident report in triplicate, complete with statements from witnesses (one copy for the school nurse, one for the principal or immediate supervisor, and one to be retained for the teacher's own file).
3. Analyze accident in view of known facts.
4. Ascertain cause of accident.
5. Set out to eliminate possibility of similar accident occurring.
6. Review safety practices and procedures.
7. Check progress of injured pupil.

Shop teachers should be completely familiar with the established procedures for taking care of accidents and injuries. If none has been established for a given school system, it would behoove the individual teacher to draw up his own for his own protection and that of his pupils. A standardized procedure will serve to relieve the anxiety of the teacher in the event of a pupil injury. The investigation, inspection, and analysis following an accident in the school shop should lead directly to corrective action. Close calls or "near misses" should always serve as a call to attention. Close calls occur frequently in the school shop and are too often soon forgotten. Minor accidents and close calls are symptoms. They should serve as a warning and should be heeded. Accidents do not just happen, they are caused!

Accident Investigation

The obvious reason for the investigation of all accidents is to find out why they happened. General opinions and rationalizations are not sufficient. The investigation of school-shop accidents must go beyond the obvious to ascertain the basic reasons and contributing factors which caused the injury. Accidents cannot be effectively stopped unless it is learned how and why they happened. It is impossible to get too much information about the causes of an accident. The circumstances leading up to, and contributing to, the accident must be identified, regardless of how involved or complex they may be. The investigating person, usually the teacher or supervisory staff member, must examine every clue thoroughly.

Accident Reporting

One of the basic weaknesses of present school-shop safety programs is the failure to keep written records of accidents. Too often considerable effort is devoted to an attempt to hush up or soft pedal a school accident, primarily to avoid criticism or to avoid legal action. A prompt and thorough report should be made of each accident. While accident reports are maintained for legal purposes, an accurate evaluation and critical analysis of the reports also can serve as a basis for an improved instructional program.

A carefully devised and supervised accident reporting system is invaluable in the overall plan of accident prevention. It is important to realize that accidents which result in a minor injury should be reported along with those which are more serious.

Difficulty often arises in determining just which pupil injuries should be recorded. Certainly all those which require a doctor's or nurse's care should be. School policy and regulations may dictate how serious an accident should be before recording it, since it may pose a seeming hardship on the teacher to record all minor scratches, cuts, or slivers which occur frequently in the school shop. For the protection of the teacher and to avoid misunderstandings which may develop, when in doubt, record it! All eye injuries should be recorded, regardless of the severity of the injury.

If a shop safety program is to be successful, records must be kept on the type and frequency of pupil accidents. These records may provide the school's legal department with the most reliable source of information available in case of a liability suit. They also vividly illustrate the seriousness of the accident problem in the school shop. The type of form to use in recording accidents is a matter of opinion. The National Safety Council recommends two: the Standard Student Accident Report Form*(26)* and the Student Accident Summary Form. To be valid, the report form should be completed as soon after the accident as practical, realizing that the teacher's first duty is to care for the injured pupil.

A state-wide reporting system is in effect in New Jersey, using a standardized form developed by the Division of Vocational Education*(27)*. For purposes of this system, a reportable accident is defined as one which results in an injury requiring treatment by a licensed medical doctor. A comprehensive accident report summary is prepared yearly and distributed to all county superintendents of schools, chief school administrators, and principals, as well as to vocational education administrators, supervisors, teachers, and teacher-educators. This report is the basis for an accident analysis of the entire state educational system.

In accident reporting, statements from eye witnesses are the most important from a legal standpoint. These can be in outline form to give the eye witness an idea of what factors are important*(28)*. It is also suggested that the eye witnesses sign statements, although it is not mandatory that they do so. Legally, they are not obligated to sign such statements.

One large metropolitan school system requires an official accident report form to be filled out in triplicate. The form is used to report all accidents involving pupils which occur while they are under the jurisdiction of the school. The triplicate copies are different in color and each has a definite purpose. The pink copy is retained by the teacher for his own files. The green copy is sent to the principal, the yellow copy to the school nurse.

---

(26) See Appendix D.

(27) See Appendix E.

(28) See Appendix F.

In this way, all responsible persons have a record of the incident.

To be more fully aware of what is taking place in our school shops, we also need a record of "near misses" or near accidents. While it might seem like busywork to a teacher, it is still a helpful procedure in developing a long-range safety program. Methods of recordkeeping must be developed which are adequate to provide a basis for accident analysis while not interfering with the learning process.

Accident Analysis

To insure maximum use of accident reports, it is essential that the accident be described in detail. The basic cause must be diagnosed before a suitable remedy can be prescribed. The real cause of an accident is sometimes other than the proximate cause and may be unrelated to shop activities. For instance, personal anxiety compounded by outside pressures, such as a pending athletic contest, difficulties in other classes, or unstable home conditions, can cause a usually reliable pupil to be injured because of lack of attention to the work at hand.

Thorough accident analysis can often pinpoint the unsafe act or condition which caused an accident. To be successful, accident prevention must be focused on eliminating the superficial as well as the basic causes. All facts of an accident must be brought out into the open and carefully analyzed. The findings can then provide the basis for knowledge needed in remedial action. The withholding of facts concerning a particular accident cannot be justified under any circumstances. A thorough analysis of all accidents occurring in the school shop will insure against repetition. School authorities and individual teachers should insist on proper analysis as in aid in protecting school personnel from liability suits growing out of pupil-injury cases. Pupils themselves should be encouraged to analyze the activities carried on in the class to determine the potential hazards represented by the equipment in use.

Summary

Teachers of shop subjects in the public schools have definite legal responsibilities with regard to accident prevention. This responsibility has been rather well defined in some of the court cases involving school-related pupil injuries. Teachers are morally responsible for the health and welfare of the pupils in their charge and legally responsible for protecting them from personal injury. Shop teachers must fulfill certain well established requirements of conduct if they expect to remain free from legal entanglements. Thus, it would appear that absence from the classroom is inadvisable, no matter how short the duration.

The protection of pupils from personal injury is one of the responsibilities that shop teachers accept when they begin teaching. This protection from injury can be classified under the general term of accident prevention. A major segment of accident prevention is a well-established safety program which includes safety instruction for the pupils. A safety program in the school shop has two prime purposes justifying its existence. One is to insure safety and prevent injury to the pupils, and the second is to prevent or reduce the possibility of legal involvement.

School-shop accidents are generally caused by unsafe conditions or unsafe acts. These can often be lessened or eliminated entirely by insisting that proper work procedures be followed at all times. The individual teacher is the main figure responsible for seeing that this is accomplished. To be successful in this venture, the teacher must enforce all safety practices in the shop by providing proper supervision. The teacher must present a positive attitude toward safe operations and set a good example by his own actions which confirms this enthusiasm for accident prevention. The ultimate aim is to educate the pupils to perform all the activities in the school shop in a safe and efficient manner.

School eye-safety legislation has been passed in 36 states and is under consideration in several others. Eye-safety legislation is in reality a means of helping a teacher help himself. If a lack of administrative support once prevented the instigation of an eye-safety program, the legislation now provides that support. Legislation in itself cannot prevent eye injuries, but it does provide a legal stimulus for the development of an adequate eye-safety program in every school.

The advent of mandatory school eye-safety legislation has added a new dimension to the ramifications of responsibility and liability. The provisions of this legislation pose some rather interesting hypotheses since they relate directly to school districts, administrators, and teachers. Would it be difficult to predict the outcome of a court action based on an eye injury in a state with eye-safety legislation on the books, but, occurring in a school without an active safety program in effect? Although the final decision is with the court, it is certain that alleged negligence would be claimed. The school district could be declared negligent by omission for failing to provide the impetus for an eye-safety program. This omission could be interpreted as a lack of foreseeability in not compensating for a recognized hazard or unsafe condition. The educational significance notwithstanding, the teacher's responsibility relates directly to the enforcement of the provisions of the legislation in the classroom and laboratory.

If the teacher fails to act, this inaction could be interpreted as a lack of foreseeability constituting the proximate cause of the resultant injury.

In general, the likelihood of accidents in the school shop can be reduced appreciably through adequate supervision and definite instructions in the use of tools, materials, and equipment. Printed rules and regulations are secondary, and can only be as effective as the emphasis that is placed on them. More specifically, the following suggestions, if thoroughly indoctrinated, will contribute toward the reduction of injury-producing accidents and the potential liability that may result.

1. The teacher must be in the classroom when class is in session.
2. All hand tools and machines must be in good working condition. The machines must be properly guarded, with the guards in place and in use whenever the machines are in operation.
3. Each pupil should be required to pass a safety test. Test results should be filed for future reference.
4. Regular inspections should be made of the tools and equipment used by the pupils.
5. Complete instructions must be given to pupils before they are allowed to operate a machine.
6. Pupils must be supervised closely to insure that the equipment is operated correctly and that instructions are being followed meticulously.
7. Safety procedures must be reviewed periodically with the entire class to prevent carelessness fostered by overconfidence or forgetfulness.
8. Insist on proper eye and face protection.
9. The immediate supervisor or administrator must be notified in writing of any unsafe conditions which cannot be remedied immediately by the teacher.
10. In the event of an accident, an accident report must be filed, complete with statements from all witnesses.
11. The shop teacher should have a knowledge of safety instructional materials.
12. A statement of the general policies for the safe conduct of the class should be prepared and kept on file.

Enforcement of the above recommendations is essential to protect an individual teacher. There are additonal precautions that teachers may take to enhance their position in this regard. These would include a knowledge of first aid, familiarity with school laws and statutes governing liability, use of locking devices on machines during the emergency of the teacher's absence from the classroom, setting a proper example for the pupils, and the realization that pupils are children and are in need of more care and guidance than adults.

Teachers should resist the temptation to treat students who become ill or who are injured while at school. Their responsibility is to obtain prompt and competent medical assistance in the event of an emergency. They are not expected to possess an expert knowledge of medicine, but are expected to act as a reasonable and prudent person untrained in the practice of medicine would act under the same or similar circumstances.

Review Questions

1. What are the primary and secondary purposes of safety instruction in the school shop?
2. What three major factors stand out as basic causes of accidents in the school shop?
3. How can a well-organized safety program be of benefit to the teacher in the event of legal action?
4. What are some of the main advantages of administering safety tests from a legal standpoint? Some of the disadvantages?
5. To protect themselves from the possibility of being declared negligent in the event of a pupil injury, what precautions must shop teachers take when called from the classroom while class is in session?
6. What legal responsibilities do shop teachers have with regard to the mechanical guarding of machines? What responsibilities does the school district have?
7. What are the four main principles of machine guarding?
8. Of what value are waiver permission statements signed by parents giving permission for their child to use power machines in the school shop?
9. What regulations govern the administration of first aid to injured pupils in your state? In your school?
10. What immediate action is required of a teacher following a pupil injury? What secondary actions should be taken?
11. How serious must a physical injury to a pupil be before it is recorded? An eye injury?
12. From a legal standpoint, what is the most important single aspect of accident reporting?

13. What legal values might an accident report contain in the event of a damage suit?
14. What are the greatest values inherent in accident analysis?
15. What is the status of school eye-safety legislation in your state?
16. Are the standards and regulations governing eye and face protection in your school adequate?
17. What is the Wise Owl Club and how can membership be attained?

CHAPTER 6

The Consequences of Liability

COMPULSORY school attendance, technological advances, and the population explosion have necessitated major changes in the public school system. Certain problems accompanied these changes and conflicts of opinion resulted. In an attempt to arrive at a logical solution to some of the problems, a train of litigation resulted. The courts, in ruling on these cases, openly influenced the direction of education. This is true in the area of teacher liability resulting from school-related pupil injuries.

In spite of teachers' continued efforts to serve the best interests of the pupils, a significant increase has been noted in the number of cases in which teachers have been sued for damages because of pupil injuries. The average sum awarded in court is reflected in the inflationary spiral. An unfavorable court decision charging an individual shop teacher or a school district with negligence could, in effect, demoralize the progressive work of our modern school system. Parents could well dissuade their children from enrolling in shop classes. Discontinuance of the shop program itself could be a possibility in some of the more serious cases.

Teachers could be charged with incompetence or neglect of duty if proved negligent. These factors constitute legal grounds for dismissal and could result in the teacher being relieved of his teaching duties. If teachers believed themselves to be potentially liable for all possible pupil injuries, they might be tempted to seek employment in a less hazardous occupation.

Any sound philosophy of education imposes on teachers and school authorities an obligation to provide for the safety and welfare of the pupils in their charge. Teacher indifference to liability and the feeling that accidents will always happen in someone else's class still constitute a major problem. Accidents in the school shop pose economic as well as humane problems. Litigation can prove costly and unpleasant, even though the shop teacher and the school district may be exonerated.

It has been established that a shop teacher can be held liable if he is proved to be negligent. In his position as a teacher, he is legally obligated to exercise that degree of care a reasonably prudent parent would exercise under the same or similar circumstances. Because of the responsibilities that are inherent in his position, a teacher must take definite steps to prevent being declared liable for a pupil injury in his class.

Recognition of the principles of law as applied to liability should in no way deter the learning process. An understanding of these principles should assist the teacher and the administration in creating the right atmosphere for learning. Legislation and insurance have proven beneficial, but cannot be expected to completely absolve the teacher from liability for acts of personal negligence. Protection of teachers does not in itself contribute to or encourage carelessness on the part of the individual teacher. Rather it tends to enhance the teacher's poise, security, and sense of well-being.

Recommendations

The following recommendations are based on the needs which are evident from a review of the problems associated with liability resulting from school-related pupil injuries. Consideration is given not only to those areas which directly affect the individual teacher, but also to those which would benefit education as a whole. Existing laws and their interpretation will not permit implementation of some of these recommendations. Others would merely require the initiative and interest of the individual teacher or, in some instances, a teachers' organization. Whatever the case, they should be given earnest consideration because of the seriousness of the problem.

Seek passage of mandatory save-harmless legislation. Legislation of this nature attempts to indemnify the teacher against financial loss and appears to be the most equitable solution to teacher liability developed to date.

Clearly define in the school laws of the state the current policy with regard to liability. The fact that the common-law principle has been abrogated in whole or in part in 27 states and the District of Columbia is evidence of change. See chart, Appendix B.

Clearly define the position of the individual teacher with regard to possible liability. States which do not by statute or school-law assign liability to the school district are governed by the principle of common-law immunity. If state statutes remain silent, it can be assumed that the teachers are legally responsible for their actions and are subject to prosecution and payment of damages for pupil injuries.

Incorporate a section relating to liability into teacher handbooks. The teacher is the main figure in the prevention of liability resulting from school-related pupil injuries. He should be cognizant of the circumstances under which liability suits have been filed and the legal framework which governs a teacher's responsibilities.

Seek legal counsel whenever legal problems are evident. Teachers and administrators are not expected to understand all of the intricacies of law which apply to the schools. Professional assistance is often needed and, for efficiency's sake, should be brought into the case early.

Have full-time physicians on the staff of the larger school districts. Full-time professional nurses should be placed in all schools of the district. A malpractice clause which protects part-time physicians and nurses should be included in the district insurance policy.

Require shop teachers to be trained in first aid and given authority to treat minor injuries. The degree of care necessary would be determined by the seriousness of the injury. A teacher must be careful to apply only that first aid which is necessary and nothing further.

Install complete first-aid kits in each school shop. The completeness or composition of any first-aid kit would be directly related to the authority to administer first aid granted to the teacher by the local school administration or by state statutes.

Require shop teachers to complete a course in industrial safety as a part of teacher training. A teacher's interest, background, and familiarity with safety factors relates directly to the safety climate of a school shop. To meet the challenge of rapid change, the schools may have to look to industry for examples, new techniques, research, and guidance.

Instigate an inservice training program on safety and liability for teachers already employed. The effectiveness of a safety program in a school shop depends to a great extent on the teacher. Difficulties often arise with teachers who don't know about safety requirements and don't know that they don't know.

Request administrators to use discretion and limit the number of students assigned to any one teacher in any one shop or laboratory. Due to the nature of the activities which are normal in a shop class, limitations of a human nature dictate a maximum number of pupils who can be handled safely and efficiently.

Adopt standards of machine guarding on a state-wide basis and rigidly enforce them on the local level. A machine, being an inanimate object, cannot distinguish a skilled, experienced worker from one who is unskilled and who lacks the experience necessary to perform an operation safely. Guarding of machines is visible evidence that the school district has satisfied its responsibility in this regard.

Keep all equipment including hand tools in good working condition. Although it is difficult to ascertain at what point or state of operation a tool or power machine becomes dangerous, regular inspection procedures will point up danger areas in need of attention.

Have shop facilities inspected periodically by recognized state industrial safety inspectors. Work areas should be regularly inspected and equipment and facilities kept in safe condition. No defective equipment should be used until the necessary repairs have been made.

Color code according to the American Standard Color Code. In addition to the increase in safety that color coding promotes, it can also make the school shop a more attractive place to work in. Equipment, machine controls, ha ardous areas, and aisles should be color coded.

Require safety tests in all activity classes. Safety tests can provide a positive record that at least some safety instruction has been given. The tests can also serve as an aid in improving the instructional process.

Work toward 100 percent eye safety in the school shop and the passage of mandatory school eye-safety legislation. Eye protection in school shops is a vitally needed and somewhat neglected phase of the safety program. Eye injuries in the schools could be almost entirely eliminated because almost all of them are preventable and can be guarded against.

Develop standardized procedures to be followed in the event of a pupil injury. It is to the advantage of the teacher to have and to follow a predetermined plan should an accident occur. A workable plan should consist of primary and secondary phases.

Require mandatory accident reports of all injuries. Accident reports are valuable in indicating points of difficulty and in providing factual data in the event of litigation. A more effective defense can be prepared if attorneys are presented with pertinent details derived from an accident report compiled immediately after an accident has occurred.

Establish and enforce a shop practice that no pupil shall use a machine or tool without the authorization of the teacher. The courts have been most severe in their criticism of administrators and teachers who expect or require pupils to perform experiments or operate certain machines which subject pupils to hazards without requiring that the strictest supervision be exercised over them.

Restrict the activities of accident-prone pupils and pupils with disabilities. The tests developed to date cannot provide conclusive evidence of individual accident proneness. There are, however, predictive qualities of possible accidents. Statistics will aid in these predictions and point out potential danger areas, the time of day accidents are most likely to occur, and specific activities that may be conducive to accidents.

Enforce strict discipline consistent with accepted methods of good teaching and in keeping with school policy. Perhaps the greatest deterrent to teacher liability is accident prevention through a well-developed and functioning safety program. If an accident can be prevented, legal action is not a possibility.

Develop criteria that rate the environmental safety of the shop. The environmental hazards which contribute to the accident toll include poor housekeeping conditions, improper working conditions, defective or poorly maintained equipment, and improper dress. The teacher has a responsibility to anticipate danger and maintain safe working conditions.

Prepare all requests for improvement of the shop environment in triplicate. One copy for the principal, one for the supervisor, and one for the permanent files of the teacher intiating the request.

Require a qualified shop teacher for substitute work in any shop class. The technical aspects of teaching industrial processes involves the use of power machines and various materials, therefore, it is mandatory that only properly trained persons be allowed to substitute in this area.

Inform parents of the normal activities carried on in shop classes. Parents have the right to know the nature of the activities their children participate in as a part of their school work.

Encourage familiarity with the history and reasons behind school laws. There should be no real conflict between the laws governing education and educational purposes. From a study of these laws and their related ramifications, a great deal may be learned about efficient techniques of supervision and administration.

Encourage alertness to the changing concepts of school law in regard to liability. Knowledge of the laws governing education should reduce the amount of indifference by teachers toward liability and make them actively eager to avoid trouble.

Investigate the possibility of liability insurance. Insurance has been advocated by many as a possible solution to liability resulting from school-related injury cases. In addition to group policies offered by state education associations, some teachers have extended their residential liability policies to include their place of employment.

Support local, state, and national professional organizations through active participation. These professional education organizations provide direction, leadership, and services which are directly beneficial to all teachers.

A Projected Solution to Teacher Liability Problems

In those states which rely on governmental immunity, the school district cannot be held liable for damages. This places the teacher in a rather precarious position, although the history of court cases involving teachers indicates a degree of commiseration on their behalf. In those states which have abrogated the principle of governmental immunity, the school district is open to suit. This can be a costly proposition for both the defendant school district and the plaintiff pupil. In those states which have save-harmless statutes in effect, action must be carried out through expensive court proceedings in order to obtain a judgment. Under save-harmless laws, the teacher receives protection from financial loss.

In times of constant change and specialization, predictions of future trends are hazardous. It does seem likely, however, that an increase in the awareness of the possibility of liability will result in a renewed effort to provide an equitable solution. The limited provisions now in effect are not adequate and have not kept pace with existing conditions. Complete abrogation of the immunity rule has met with opposition from the courts and school personnel alike. To date, save-harmless laws are perhaps the most logical and effective solution. When the general public becomes fully aware that a teacher is financially backed by the school district under these laws, however, new problems may arise.

The solution to the problem of liability for school-related pupil injuries does not lie entirely in providing more legislative protection for teachers and school districts but in apportioning more responsibility to them. If they can be held more accountable for accidents, greater care and concern on their part will be the result. They are more likely to get to the source of the problem which has, as its basic premise, the prevention of injury-causing accidents. The initiative for this action must come from the teachers themselves and the school district. Contained in this action would be greater care in the selection of teachers, the provision of more adequate facilities, reevaluation of the methods of teaching, and more rigid standards with regard to the care and maintenance of physical facilities.

Many of the laws governing public school education are steeped in antiquity. Those related to liability for school-related pupil injuries are no exception. Many of the reasons advanced at the time of their inception are not as sound today as they were when they were enacted. In his first annual message delivered December 3, 1861, Abraham Lincoln is quoted as saying, "It is as much the duty of government to render proper justice against itself, in favor of its citizens, as to administer the same between private individuals." It would seem from an analysis of this statement that Lincoln himself would have opposed governmental immunity for school districts as such, and would have supported some plan by which injured pupils could receive some compensation.

Pupil Compensation—A Proposal

Industry has long recognized the fact that there are certain unavoidable accidents. In spite of the many improvements made in working conditions, a certain percentage of these accidents is likely to continue. The individual workman who is injured in the course of his employment is protected by workmen's compensation laws. These laws provide compensation, in lieu of wages, for an injured employee regardless of fault. The victim of an on-the-job accident can usually recover damages from his employer without initiating legal action against him. Workmen's compensation is based on the principle that the financial burden associated with an industrial injury should be borne by industry rather than by the injured.

It is rather difficult, under existing conditions, for pupils who are injured while pursuing an education in the public schools to realize any damages. One of the main reasons is that funds have not been made specifically available for this purpose. Compensating the injured pupil is an important public responsibility, however, regardless of the source from which payment might have to come. A protection plan of some sort of financial assistance is needed to provide medical care for injured pupils.

A modified form of workmen's compensation involving pupil remuneration could be a solution to the problem of liability associated with school-related injuries. This would directly benefit the injured pupil and could parallel the provisions made by industry. Legal action against the teacher and the school district would be prohibited by statute under a plan of this type. An equitable plan would require school districts by statute to remunerate pupils for all school-connected injuries, except those which are willfully self-inflicted. The scale of compensation would of necessity be more flexible for school-related injuries than for industrial injuries. Medical care would be completely covered, and disabling injuries would be prorated in accordance with the future earning power of the injured pupil.

School districts implementing a plan of pupil compensation would utilize their discretionary powers in the purchase of insurance from a company approved by the state insurance commission. Rates for this insurance would be assigned according to the number of participants and the frequency of accidents within a given school district. Higher rates would be assigned to those school districts which have a high accident rate and those who fail to provide safe working conditions. It is assumed that a direct result of this plan would be a tightening up of the rules and regulations governing potentially hazardous activities in the school. School authorities would be more conscientious in their attempts to study the causes of accidents and institute preventative measures.

The school district itself deserves a degree of protection because of the vital function it serves in our society. At the same time, it must be made to feel the responsibility for the care of the pupils under its jurisdiction. Complete abrogation of the principle of governmental immunity, which allows suit against school districts, can be costly. Under a plan of pupil compensation, governmental immunity of school districts would be enforced by legislation and correlated with an equitable method of compensation for injured pupils.

The Suggested Pupil Compensation Plan

A well-founded plan of pupil compensation for school-related injuries would serve to take the guesswork and uncertainty out of this phase of school activity. At present, no two states are in complete accord in the handling and enforcement of school-related liability cases. One thing that is definite in all states is that liability cases are costly and disagreeable at best. A stable compensation plan would rule out the possibility of costly court trials. It would also help to provide a feeling of more financial security for the teacher, because he would know that his entire life's earnings would not be in jeopardy in the event of a serious accident in his classroom. A standardization of procedures in handling the compensation for injuries would aid public education in all states and keep misunderstandings and misinterpretations at a minimum.

Direct purchase of insurance could be made, or else it would be possible to administer a plan of pupil compensation on a state-wide basis with the state department of education acting as a self-insurer for the entire state. This would be of direct benefit to smaller schools with a limited student body and a limited budget. Payments into a state-wide compensation fund would be based on a prorated average of the number of pupils in attendance in each school district. To be successful, participation would be compulsory for all public schools in the state. A compensation plan of this type would directly affect public relations between the school and parents. Parents will tend to be more liberal in allowing their children to participate in all of the activities sponsored by the school if they are fully informed as to the mechanics of operation of such a plan.

This proposed plan of pupil compensation is no panacea. Rather, it is an attempt to provide some stimulus and to encourage intelligent thinking in the development of an effective, humane, and economical solution to the problem of liability resulting from school-related injury cases. There are many inconsistencies and restrictions to be resolved, but it is felt that the advantages will outweigh the disadvantages. The plan is designed to assist the unfortunate pupil who is injured and to relieve the teacher of direct liability. How nearly these objectives could be accomplished can only be determined through continued research and actual implementation. The legality of inaugurating such a plan would rest with state legislative action or rely on a ruling by the attorney general in each state.

Many educators feel that a plan of pupil compensation might result in a deluge of claims, for both past and present injuries. To compensate for this, rigid legal controls would have to be in force immediately on inception. These controls would lawfully prohibit retroactive claims based on past injuries.

Summary

Liability for school districts, school administrators, and teachers may emanate from several sources. The most discernable is that which arises as a result of torts. A school district may be obligated to compensate a person for injury or loss resulting from a tort committed by a school administrator or teacher. Individuals, including school administrators, but most frequently teachers, may be personally liable for torts committed within the course or scope of their employment.

Negligence is associated with the law of torts. Liability for torts arises from negligence which may be defined as failure to exercise the degree of care for the safety and well-being of others that a reasonable and prudent person would have exercised under the same or similiar circumstances. Thus an important test for negligence is "What course of action would a reasonable person have followed?" The burden of proving negligence rests with the plaintiff, while the existence of negligence and the amount of compensable damage arising therefrom are questions to be decided by the court. Germane in the assessment of negligence are the predominant elements of proximate cause and foreseeability. Other factors are likely to be considered but these are by far the most pertinent.

Case law and legislation have influenced the field of school law as it affects liability. Principles of law have changed as a result of a court decision or an act of the legislature. This is particularly true with respect to the gradual erosion of the common-law doctrine. Save-harmless statutes have been one of the more positive outgrowths of the dissatisfaction with the immunity syndrome. Judicial abrogation has been more widespread in recent years. The common-law doctrine, long influenced by the idea that the "King Can Do No Wrong," has been replaced by a body of law assuring an individual consideration for redress following a negligent act. The "Men of Devon" belong to another age. This bit of case law, after having served with distinction for more than 150 years, is now considered a time-honored classic.

The actual number and/or percentage of shop-related student injuries resulting in a court action is difficult to assess. An even more difficult task is determining the percentage that culminate as cases of record. Nationwide there does not appear to be a defined pattern. Of the 72 cases of record reviewed, 33 were decided in favor of the plaintiff (student or family member), 32 in favor of the defendant (teacher and/or school district), and 7 were remanded. California and New York have each contributed 15 decisions or a combined total of 42 percent. The period 1970-80 reflects a social metamorphosis in that for the first time in history two of the cases examined resulted from injuries sustained by teenage girls. The realization that 25 states are free from a case of record resulting from a school-shop accident is of little solace in our unpredictable and changing society. The threat of litigation is unmistakable when an injury occurs.

Eye protection for students participating in activities posing exposure to eye hazards has been a continuing objective of educators. Enforcement, however, has been a matter of personal concern with few standards governing the selection of protective equipment. Eye safety as it relates to the public schools took on new meaning in 1963 with the passage of the Ohio Eye Safety Law. This law mandated the use of face and eye protection for specific activities. Now all eye protection equipment must meet the standards of the American National Standards Institute (ANSI) Code Z87.1-1968-1979 and subsequent revisions thereof. The passage of eye safety legislation has prompted educators to take an interest in other facets of safety, including the development and implementation of statewide safety programs and accident reporting systems.

Education should follow the lead of business and industry in attempting to make the school shop not only a safe place to work, but a safe place to learn how to work. Although public schools are not generally considered major targets for OSHA, a comprehensive safety program can serve as an effective vehicle in dealing with potential liability. Compliance with

OSHA regulations would be a distinct advantage should litigation be brought against a teacher and/or a school district. OSHA regulations have served to spotlight other local, state, and federal codes of conduct relating to safety and health. OSHA, however, does not have total acceptance throughout the nation's work force. The disillusionment of business and industry may have a bearing on whether or not OSHA becomes effectual in all states.

The progress of education in our modern schools is swift. To keep up, we must act, and act soon, before additional damage is done. To be effective, it will require a concentrated effort by those who are interested in a practical solution. Action must be the byword as lip service alone will not accomplish the task. Teachers of shop subjects should put into practice a strong safety program and become aware of their legal rights and responsibilities with reference to the liability of pupils. A shop teacher who remains in the classroom while the class is in session, who properly instructs and supervises pupils in the use of materials, tools, and machines, who maintains a functional safety program, and who has the welfare of the pupils at heart should have little fear of liability.

When you analyze the merits of your own safety program, consider one of Sir Winston Churchill's wartime memos which read, "Pray do not let it be thought that you are satisfied with such a result. If you simply take up the attitude of defending it, there will be no hope of improvement."

APPENDIX A

Glossary

Abrogate. To annul, repeal, or destroy an order or rule issued by a subordinate authority; to repeal a former law by legislative act, or by usage.

Accident. An event which takes place without one's foresight or expectation; a mishap resulting in injury to a person or damage to a thing.

Action. To bring legal action against another for the protection of a right or the redress of a wrong.

Allegation. A statement by a party of what he undertakes to prove.

Allege. To state positively but without proof; to make an allegation.

ANSI. American National Standards Institute.

Assumption of risk. Assumes knowledge of danger and the extent of its complications; a pupil being aware of the risk involved and making a voluntary choice to encounter it.

Case law. Has its source in judicial opinions based primarily on interpretations of constitutional law and statutory law and the application of common-law principles.

Citation. Reference to law books; includes the book where the reference is found, the volume number, and section or page number.

Common law. The first primary source of law, based on judicial precedents and previous court decisions.

Comparative negligence. Whereby damages would be divided on a basis of a comparison of faults involved in causing an injury.

Contributory negligence. Any want of ordinary care on the part of the person injured which combined and concurred with the defendant's negligence, contributed to the injury as a proximate cause thereof, and as an element without which the injury would not have occurred.

Court of record. The appellate or highest court in any given state.

Damages. The financial or monetary compensation awarded in court to the person who has suffered injury through the unlawful act, omission, or negligence of another.

Defendant. The party against whom relief or recovery is sought in a court action.

Defense. That which is offered and alleged by the defendant as reason why the plaintiff should not recover damages.

Demurrer. A pleading which, assuming the truth of the matter alleged by the opposite party, sets up that it is insufficient in law, or that there is some other defect on the face of the pleadings constituting a legal reason why the opposing party should not be allowed to proceed further.

Disclaimer. A refusal or renunciation of a responsibility or claim; a document formally renouncing a claim.

Discretionary power. The power to do or refrain from doing a certain thing; one which is not imperative; controlled by individual judgment.

Dissenting opinion. Nonagreement with the conclusions held by the majority of a court.

Factual cause. The obvious, evident, or plainly understood cause of an accident.

Foreseeability. The ability to anticipate hazardous situations or potential accident causes; the first test in determining whether or not there was negligence.

Governmental immunity. Immunity from tort actions enjoyed by governmental subdivisions in common-law states.

Impunity. Freedom from punishment, injury, or loss.

Indemnify. To save harmless; to secure against loss or damage; to protect or insure against financial loss.

In loco parentis. In the place of the parent and being charged with some of the parents' rights, responsibilities, and duties.

Intervening cause. The negligent acts of a third party which serve to break the chain of causation between the accident and the alleged negligence of the defendant.

Judgment. Decision of the court, usually involving the payment of damages.

Judicial. Of, pertaining to, or appropriate to, the administration of justice, courts of justice, a judge thereof, or the proceedings therein.

Legal cause. That harm-producing cause but for which the injury would not have occurred in the natural sequence of events.

Liability. Legal responsibility; the state of one who is bound in law and justice to do something which may be enforced by action.

Litigant. One engaged in a lawsuit.

Litigation. The act or process of carrying on a lawsuit.

Majority opinion. Statement of reasons for the views of the majority in a decision in which some members of the court disagree.

Malfeasance. The performance of an act that is wrongful and unlawful; a comprehensive term including any wrongful conduct that affects, interrupts, or interferes with the performance of official duties.

Misfeasance. The performance of a lawful action in an illegal or improper manner.

Negate. To deny or nullify; to declare or prove nonexistent.

Negligence. The omission of doing something which a reasonable man, guided by those normal considerations which ordinarily regulate human affairs, would do; or the doing of something which a reasonable or prudent man would not do.

Nonfeasance. The neglect or omission of some duty which a person is expected or legally bound to perform.

OSHA. Occupational Safety and Health Act of 1970 (Public Law 91-596).

Plaintiff. The person who brings an action; he who sues by filing a complaint.

Plea. The defendant's response to the charges in a lawsuit.

Pleadings. The successive written allegations of the parties in a suit at law or equity designed to disclose to the court or jury the real matter in dispute.

Precedent. A judicial decision, or a form of proceeding, or course of action, that serves as a rule for future determinations in similar or analogous cases; an authority to be followed in courts of justice.

Proprietary duties. Those duties relating to the primary responsibility of a municipality or governmental subdivision which are not considered governmental duties.

Proprietary rights. Those rights which an owner of property has by virtue of his ownership.

Proximate cause. That which, in the natural and continual sequence, unbroken by any efficient intervening cause, produces the injury and without which the result would not have occurred.

Redress. To make amends as for a loss; to relieve of anything unjust; reparation of a wrong.

Remand. To return a case to the court from which it came for further proceedings following an appellate decision.

Res ipsa loquitur. The act or thing speaks for itself.

Respondeat superior. Master-servant rule. A vicarious liability of an employer in which he is held responsible for the negligence of his employees.

Safe-place statutes. Statutes which provide that every owner of a public building shall so construct it as to render it safe.

Save-harmless laws. Laws which require school districts to defend and to pay judgments rendered against teachers who have been held personally liable for injuries sustained by pupils as the result of the teacher's negligence.

Shop teacher. A qualified professional person responsible for the instruction of pupils in the types of education related to industry, including industrial-arts, technical, and vocational-industrial education.

Stare decisis. When a court has made a declaration of a legal principle, it is the law until changed by competent authority.

Statute. An act of the legislature.

Statutes of limitation. Statutes which restrict the amount of time that may elapse between an accidental injury and the filing of a notice of claim or damage suit.

Statutory law. The second primary source of law which consists of the statutes enacted by the legislature of any sovereign state.

Tort. Legal wrong committed on the person or property of another, independent of contract.

Ultra vires. Acts beyond the scope of authority.

Waive. To renounce, set aside, or relinquish voluntarily, as a right which one may enforce if he chooses.

APPENDIX B

State Regulations Relating to Teacher Liability

State	Common-Law Immunity	Common-Law Abrogated	Save-Harmless Laws	Comparative Negligence (apportionment of damages)	Statutes of Limitations	Educator's Professional Liability Insurance with Amount of Coverage	Number of Cases of Court Record						Remarks
							1920-1929	1930-1939	1940-1949	1950-1959	1960-1969	1970-1980	
Alabama	X					$1,000,000							State employees held exempt from tort liabilities.
Alaska		X				$1,000,000							School district and the city are one legal entity.
Arizona		X				$1,000,000					1		Common-law immunity abrogated by Supreme Court.
Arkansas	X			X		$1,000,000							School districts allowed to provide legal counsel.
California		X	X		X	$1,000,000		7	1	5	2		Legislation making districts liable for negligent acts of employees.
Colorado		X				$1,000,000							Common-law immunity abrogated by Supreme Court.
Connecticut		X	X										Common-law immunity abrogated by legislative action.
Delaware	X					$1,000,000							
District of Columbia		X									1		All legal actions referred to the Corporation Counsel.
Florida		X				$1,000,000			1				

State	*Common-Law Immunity*	*Common-Law Abrogated*	*Save-Harmless Laws*	*Comparative Negligence (apportionment of damages)*	*Statutes of Limitations*	*Educator's Professional Liability Insurance with Amount of Coverage*	*Number of Cases of Court Record* 1920-1929	1930-1939	1940-1949	1950-1959	1960-1969	1970-1980	*Remarks*
Georgia	X			X		$1,000,000	1						School districts authorized to carry liability insurance.
Hawaii		X			X	$1,000,000							Teachers not laible to suit–Tort Liability Act of 1957.
Idaho		X				$1,000,000							
Illinois		X				$1,000,000						1	Governmental employees tort immunity does not apply.
Indiana		X				$1,000,000						2	
Iowa		X	X			$1,000,000							Comprehensive statute abolishing common-law immunity & creating save-harmless law.
Kansas	X					$1,000,000							Common-law immunity upheld.
Kentucky		X				$1,000,000							Liability insurance provided for staff by school boards.
Louisiana		X				$1,000,000						1	Court of Appeals held school boards not immune from suit.
Maine	X		X			$1,000,000			1				
Maryland	X					$1,000,000						1	Sovereign immunity upheld as it applies to public schools.
Massachusetts	X		X			$1,000,000		1				1	Supreme Court "intends" to abrogate municipal immunity.
Michigan		X				$1,000,000							Safe-place statutes in effect which include schools.
Minnesota		X	X	X		$1,000,000						1	Comparative negligence decreed in case of court record.
Mississippi	X			X		$1,000,000							

State	Common-Law Immunity	Common-Law Abrogated	Save-Harmless Laws	Comparative Negligence (apportionment of damages)	Statutes of Limitations	Educator's Professional Liability Insurance with Amount of Coverage	Number of Cases of Court Record						Remarks
							1920-1929	1930-1939	1940-1949	1950-1959	1960-1969	1970-1980	
Missouri		X				$1,000,000							Common-law immunity abrogated by Supreme Court.
Montana	X					$1,000,000							
Nebraska		X		X		$1,000,000						1	Common-law immunity abrogated by Supreme Court.
Nevada		X			X	$1,000,000					1		Six-month statute of limitation in effect.
N. Hampshire	X					$1,000,000							
New Jersey		X	X					1		1		1	School boards may arrange & maintain proper insurance.
New Mexico	X					$1,000,000							
New York		X	X		X		3		7	3		2	Ruled that negligence may be imputed to school boards.
N. Carolina	X				X	$1,000,000						1	Tort Claims Act. Hearings are held by Industrial Commission.
N. Dakota	X					$1,000,000							School districts authorized to obtain liability insurance.
Ohio	X					$1,000,000	1					1	Immunity covers school but not teachers.
Oklahoma		X				$1,000,000							Immunity waived to the extent of liability insurance.
Oregon		X				$1,000,000							"Wrongful Act" protection in professional liability policy.
Pennsylvania		X				$1,000,000			1	2		1	School districts maintain complete autonomy.
Rhode Island		X	X			$1,000,000							Student teachers included under save-harmless statute.

State	*Common-Law Immunity*	*Common-Law Abrogated*	*Save-Harmless Laws*	*Comparative Negligence (apportionment of damages)*	*Statutes of Limitations*	*Educator's Professional Liability Insurance with Amount of Coverage*	*Number of Cases of Court Record*						*Remarks*
							1920-1929	*1930-1939*	*1940-1949*	*1950-1959*	*1960-1969*	*1970-1980*	
S. Carolina	X					$1,000,000						1	
S. Dakota	X			X		$1,000,000							
Tennessee	X			X		$1,000,000							Recovery permitted up to amount of insurance coverage.
Texas	X					$1,000,000					1		Professional Employees Immunity Statute in effect.
Utah		X				$1,000,000					1	1	Statute authorizes boards to sue and be sued.
Vermont	X		X			$1,000,000							Save-harmless coverage on all employees.
Virginia	X					$1,000,000					1		Court ruled that immunity does not apply to teachers.
Washington		X			X	$1,000,000	1	2	1		2		Common-law sustained for school shop related injuries.
W. Virginia	X					$1,000,000	1						Purchase of liability insurance not authorized by statute governing school boards.
Wisconsin		X		X	X	$1,000,000	1		1	1	2		Comparative negligence has replaced contributory negligence.
Wyoming	X		X			$1,000,000							Permissive save-harmless laws in effect.
TOTALS							8	11	13	12	12	16	=72

APPENDIX C

Cases of Court Record Resulting from Pupil Injuries in the School Shop

Case	Decision
ARIZONA	
Morris v. *Ortiz and School District No. 1 of Pima County* 437 P.2d 652. 1968	Defendant
CALIFORNIA	
Ahern v. *Livermore Union High School* 284 P.1105. 1930	Plaintiff
Calandri v. *Ione Unified School District of Amador County* 33 Cal. Rptr. 333. 1963	Plaintiff
Dutcher v. *City of Santa Rosa High School District* 290 P.2d 316. 1957	Plaintiff
Furtado v. *Montebello Unified School District* 23 Cal. Rptr. 476. 1962	Plaintiff
Goodman v. *Pasadena City High School District* 40 P.2d 854. 1935	Defendant
Grover v. *San Mateo Junior College District of San Mateo County*, 303 P.2d 602. 1956	Plaintiff
Henry v. *Garden Grove Union High School* 7 P.2d 192. 1932	Plaintiff
Klenzendorf v. *Shasta Union High School District* 40 P.2d 878. 1935	Defendant
Lehmann v. *Los Angeles City Board of Education* 316 P.2d 55. 1957	Plaintiff
Lilienthal v. *San Leandro Unified School District* 298 P.2d 889. 1956	Plaintiff

Meade v. *Oakland High School District of Alameda County*, 298 P. 987. 1931	Plaintiff
Perumeau v. *Willis* 67 P.2d 96. 1937	Defendant
Ridge v. *Boulder Creek* 140 P.2d 990. 1943	Plaintiff
Ross v. *San Francisco Unified School District* 260 P.2d 663. 1953	Plaintiff
Woodman v. *Hemet Union High School District* 29 P.2d 257. 1934	Plaintiff

DISTRICT OF COLUMBIA

Butler v. *District of Columbia* 417 F.2d 1150. 1969	Defendant

FLORIDA

Bragg v. *Board of Public Instruction of Duval County* 36 S.2d 222. 1948	Defendant

GEORGIA

Nabell v. *City of Atlanta* 126 S.E. 905. 1925	Defendant

ILLINOIS

Matteucci v. *High School District No. 208, County of Cook* 281 N.E.2d 383. 1972	Plaintiff

INDIANA

Scott County School District #1 v. *Asher* 312 N.E.2d 131. 1974	Plaintiff
South Ripley Community School Corporation v. *Peters and Powermatic-Houdaille, Inc.* 396 N.E.2d 144. 1979	Plaintiff

LOUISIANA

Danos v. *Foret, et al.* 354 S.2d 667. 1977	Plaintiff

MAINE

Brooks v. *Jacobs* 31 A.2d 414. 1943	Plaintiff

MARYLAND

Duncan v. *Koustenis* 271 A.2d 547. 1970	Remanded

MASSACHUSETTS

Case	Decision
Fulgoni v. *Johnston* 19 N.E.2d. 542. 1939	Defendant
Oeschger v. *Fitzgerald* 314 N.E.2d 444. 1974	Remanded

MINNESOTA

Case	Decision
Scott v. *Independent School District #709, Duluth* 256 N.W.2d 485. 1977	Plaintiff

NEBRASKA

Case	Decision
Miles v. *School District #138 of Cheyenne County* 281 N.W.2d 396. 1979	Defendant

NEVADA

Case	Decision
Kaminski v. *Woodbury* 462 P.2d 45. 1969	Remanded

NEW JERSEY

Case	Decision
Cadmus v. *Long Branch Board of Education* 382 A.2d 98. 1977	Defendant
Meyer v. *Board of Education, Middletown* 86 A.2d 761. 1952	Defendant
Taylor v. *Kevlin* 1 A.2d 433. 1938	Defendant

NEW YORK

Case	Decision
Daigneault v. *Board of Education of City of Cohoes* 179 N.Y.S.2d 331. 1958	Plaintiff
DeBenedittis v. *Board of Education of New York City* 67 N.Y.S.2d 30. 1946	Plaintiff
Edkins v. *Board of Education of New York City* 41 N.E.2d 75. 1942	Plaintiff
Ford v. *Board of Education* 194 N.Y.S. 934. 1922	Plaintiff
Govel v. *Board of Education of City of Albany* 60 N.E.2d 133. 1944	Plaintiff
Herman v. *Board of Education of Union School District 8,* 137 N.E. 24. 1922	Plaintiff
Johnson v. *Board of Education of City of Hudson* 206 N.Y.S. 610. 1924	Defendant
Ohman v. *Board of Education of New York City* 90 N.E.2d 474. 1949	Defendant

Osborn v. *Board of Education of Marathon Central School District No. 1 of Freetown* — Plaintiff
172 N.Y.S.2d 453. 1958

Reeder v. *Board of Education of New York City* — Plaintiff
50 N.E.2d 236. 1943

Ressel v. *Board of Education of the Greater Amsterdam School District* — Defendant
395 N.Y.S.2d 263. 1977

Segal v. *State of New York and the State University of New York College at Purchase* — Defendant
359 N.Y.S.2d 498. 1974

Sigman v. *Board of Education of New York City* — Defendant
97 N.Y.S.2d 302. 1950

Thomas v. *City of New York* — Plaintiff
35 N.E.2d 617. 1941

Weber v. *State of New York* — Plaintiff
53 N.Y.S.2d 598. 1945

NORTH CAROLINA

Kiser v. *Snyder, et al.* — Defendant
194 S.E.2d 638. 1973
205 S.E.2d 619. 1974

OHIO

Conrad v. *Board of Education of Ridgeville Township* — Plaintiff
163 N.E. 567. 1928

Salyers v. *Burkhart* — Remanded
352 N.E.2d 156. 1974
339 N.E.2d 652. 1975

PENNSYLVANIA

Ayala v. *Philadelphia Board of Public Education* — Remanded
305 A.2d 877. 1973

Golish v. *School District of Borough of Windber* — Defendant
15 Som. 125. 1950

Hess v. *School District of City of Harrisburg* — Defendant
69 Dauph. 77. 1956

Wilcox v. *Dunmore School District* — Defendant
43 Lack. Jur. 13. 1941

SOUTH CAROLINA

Hammond v. *Scott* — Defendant
232 S.E.2d 336. 1977

TEXAS

Case	Result
Sewell v. *London* 371 S.W.2d 426. 1963	Remanded

UTAH

Case	Result
Campbell v. *Board of Education* 389 P.2d 464. 1964	Defendant
Scott v. *School Board of Granite School District* 568 P.2d 746. 1977	Remanded

VIRGINIA

Case	Result
Crabbe v. *County School Board of Northumberland County,* 164 S.E.2d 639. 1968	Defendant

WASHINGTON

Case	Result
Babcock v. *School District No. 17 of Clallam County* 358 P.2d 547. 1961	Defendant
Banks v. *Seattle School District No. 1* 80 P.2d 835. 1938	Plaintiff
Boman v. *Union High School District No. 1, Kitsap County,* 22 P.2d 991. 1933	Plaintiff
Casper v. *Longview School District No. 122* 105 P.2d 503. 1940	Defendant
Swanson v. *School District No. 15 Pierce County* 187 P.386. 1920	Defendant
Swartley v. *Seattle School District #1* 421 P.2d 1009. 1966	Plaintiff

WEST VIRGINIA

Case	Result
Krutili v. *Board of Education of Butler District* 129 S.E.486. 1925	Defendant

WISCONSIN

Case	Result
Grosso v. *Witteman* 62 N.W.2d 386. 1954	Defendant
Kirchoff v. *City of Janesville* 38 N.W.2d 698. 1949	Defendant
Neidfelt v. *Joint School District No. 1 of City of Viroqua* 127 N.W.2d 800. 1964	Defendant
Severson v. *City of Beloit* 167 N.W.2d 258. 1969	Plaintiff
Sullivan v. *School District No. 1 of City of Tomah* 191 N.W.1020. 1923	Defendant

APPENDIX D

Standard Student Accident Report Form (NSC)

A COPY of the recommended *Standard Student Accident Report Form* (National Safety Council—Form School 1, stock number 429.21) is shown on the next page. The instructions for filling out the form are on the following page.

In addition to this form, a *Student Accident Summary Form* (National Safety Council—Form School 2M, stock number 429.22-1 for boys; Form School 2F, stock number 429.22-2 for girls) and an *Annual Student Accident Summary* (National Safety Council—Form School 3M, stock number 1001.56 for boys; Form 3F, stock number 1001.57 for girls) as well as a five-page attachment *How to Secure National Safety Council Materials to Start Standard Student Accident Reporting* are all available from the National Safety Council, 425 North Michigan Ave., Chicago, Illinois 60611.

Also available from the National Safety Council is a 34-page booklet *Student Accident Reporting Guidebook,* which gives details on how school administrators and safety supervisors can improve their safety education program through effective accident reporting. Cost of the Guidebook (40M46602, stock number 1001-20) is $1.00.

(check one)
☐ School Jurisdictional
☐ Non-School Jurisdictional

RECOMMENDED STANDARD STUDENT ACCIDENT REPORT

(See instructions on reverse side)

(check one)
Recordable ☐
Reportable Only ☐

School District:
City, State:

General

1. Name			2. Address
3. School	4. Sex Male ☐ Female ☐	5. Age	6. Grade/Special Program

7. Time Accident Occurred
Date: Day of Week: Exact Time: AM ☐ PM ☐

Injury

8. Nature of Injury

9. Part of Body Injured

10. Degree of Injury (check one)
Death ☐ Permanent ☐ Temporary (lost time) ☐ Non-Disabling (no lost time) ☐

11. Days Lost
From School: From Activities Other Than School: Total:

12. Cause of Injury

Accident

13. Accident Jurisdiction (check one)
School: Grounds ☐ Building ☐ To and From ☐ Other Activities Not on School Property ☐
Non-School: Home ☐ Other ☐

14. Location of Accident (be specific)	15. Activity of Person (be specific)
16. Status of Activity	17. Supervision (if yes, give title & name of supervisor) Yes ☐ No ☐
18. Agency Involved	19. Unsafe Act
20. Unsafe Mechanical/Physical Condition	21. Unsafe Personal Factor

22. Corrective Action Taken or Recommended

23. Property Damage
School $ Non-School $ Total $

24. Description (Give a word picture of the accident, explaining who, what, when, why and how)

Signature

25. Date of Report	26. Report Prepared by (signature & title)
27. Principal's Signature	

This form is recommended for securing data for accident prevention and safety education. School districts may reproduce this form adding space for optional data. Reference: *Student Accident Reporting Guidebook*, National Safety Council, 425 N. Michigan Avenue, Chicago, Illinois 60611. 1966. 34 pages.

INSTRUCTIONS

Please read carefully — Fill out form completely

Use the form on the reverse side to report each school and each non-school jurisdictional accident. In the upper left corner, check appropriate box:

School Jurisdictional. Any accident which results in any injury to a pupil and/or property damage which occurs in a school building, on school grounds, on the way to or from school, or in connection with any other school-sponsored activity even though not on school property.

Non-School Jurisdictional. An accident which causes restriction of activity to the pupil, occurring anywhere not definitely specified above.

In the upper right corner, check appropriate box:

Recordable. If the accident results in

a. Pupil injuries severe enough to cause the loss of one-half day or more of school time, or

b. Pupil injuries severe enough to cause the loss of one-half day or more of pupil activity during non-school time, or

c. Any property damage as a result of a school jurisdictional accident.

Reportable Only. If the accident does *not* cause a *lost time* injury or property damage.

NOTE: Only those forms checked **Recordable** are to be included in the *Annual Student Accident Summary* forms which are submitted to the National Safety Council.

1. **Name.** Name of injured student.

2. **Address.** Home address.

3. **School.** School attended.

4. **Sex.** Check box.

5. **Age.** Age of student at last birthday.

6. **Grade/Special Program.** Grade level such as K—for kindergarten, 1—for first grade, 2—for second grade, etc.; Special Education, Adult Education, Junior College, etc. If a special program, such as Head Start, Student Work Program, Adult Re-Training or Pre-Primary, so indicate.

7. **Time Accident Occurred.** Indicate the time the accident occurred as follows: Date (month, day of the month, and year); day of the week; the exact time and check AM or PM.

8. **Nature of Injury.** Indicate, *to the best of your knowledge*, what the injury was, such as burn, fracture, abrasion, etc. If multiple injuries, so indicate and list each.

9. **Part of Body Injured.** Indicate part of body injured, such as lower left arm, right ankle, scalp, etc. If more than one part of body is injured, indicate as "multiple" and list each part.

10. **Degree of Injury.** Check one box. If the degree of injury is not immediately known, estimate or use a follow-up system. Reports should not be held up for lack of this information.

Death. If fatal.

Permanent. If injury results in a complete loss of, or loss of use of, a body part or parts, such as the loss of an eye, the loss of use of a limb, amputation of a part of the body, etc.

Temporary (lost time). If the injury does not cause permanent disability, but causes the child to lose one-half day or more of school, or one-half day or more of normal activity, during a non-school period.

Non-Disabling (no lost time). If the injury did not cause permanent disability and/or lost time, or loss of activity.

11. **Days Lost.** Indicate from one-half or more, the number of days that the student was absent from school; and/or the number of days from one-half day or more, the student was restricted from normal activities if during a non-school period. One-half day's lost time in school is defined as one-half of the normal school day for that particular student. The time charge for death is 1,200 days. See *Guidebook*, page 24, for permanent disability charges. If lost time is not immediately known, estimate or use a follow-up system. Reports should not be held up for lack of this information.

12. **Cause of Injury.** Identify the event which resulted in the injury, such as "struck against moving object," "fall from elevation," "rubbed or abraided," "over-exertion," etc.

13. **Accident Jurisdiction.** Check one box to indicate where the accident occurred.

14. **Location of Accident.** Indicate exact location of the accident. Example: Second floor corridor near room 210, girls' gymnasium, sidewalk at northeast corner of 12th and Locust, inside stairway at home, etc.

15. **Activity of Person.** Indicate what person was doing at time of the accident. Example: Conducting a science experiment, playing second base in soft ball, riding as a passenger in parents' car, driving a bicycle, etc.

16. **Status of Activity.** Indicate status of activity at time of the accident. Example: Regular classroom period, physical education class, intramural athletic practice, interscholastic athletics, recess, lunch period, supervised before or after school activities, at a friend's home, in the kitchen, at a supermarket, etc.

17. **Supervision.** Check box to indicate whether an adult was present at the scene of the accident; if "yes," indicate by name and title whether this adult was the teacher, another school employee, the parent, another adult, etc.

18. **Agency Involved.** Indicate the equipment, substance, material, or the thing most closely related to the accident. Example: Glass test tube, motorcycle, ground surface, other person, dog, etc.

19. **Unsafe Act.** Indicate any act on the part of the person or persons involved which may have caused or contributed to the accident. Example: Using equipment unsafely, feet in aisle, body contact in sports or other action in excess of intent of rule, not following established rules, etc.

20. **Unsafe Mechanical/Physical Condition.** Indicate any unsafe mechanical or physical conditions such as deep ruts in play area, ice on sidewalk, improperly guarded machine, improperly stored material, poor lighting, porch railing in need of repair, etc.

21. **Unsafe Personal Factor.** Indicate any unsafe personal factors that may have contributed to the accident. Example: Bodily defects such as defective hearing; lack of knowledge, skill or experience, such as failure to recognize hazards; emotional upsets such as death in the family, new sibling, parental separation or school failure.

22. **Corrective Action Taken or Recommended.** Indicate what action was taken locally and/or what further action is recommended, if needed action cannot be taken by local school personnel. Example: Maintenance action such as play area holes were filled and leveled; procedural action such as a study is being made to improve the flow of students into the auditorium; engineering recommendation such as the ventilating system should be studied to determine if sufficient for the area involved; curriculum recommendation such as the present course of study for woodworking shop should be reviewed to insure that safe procedures are included; counseling action such as referred child to guidance department.

23. **Property Damage.** Estimate in dollars the amount of damage, if any, to school property and/or other property as the result of the accident. Do not hold up report for this information. If there was no property damage write "none."

24. **Description.** Give a *word* picture of the accident, explaining who, what, where, when, why and how of the accident. Include such items as weather, equipment, unsafe conditions, unsafe acts, personal factors, and whether other persons may have contributed to the accident, and how.

25. **Date of Report.** Date report was completed.

26. **Report Prepared by.** Signature and title of person preparing report.

27. **Principal's Signature.**

APPENDIX E

Accident Report Form

NJDE 523-5 (11/77)

DIVISION USE ONLY
County Code______
LEA Code_________
School Code______

STATE OF NEW JERSEY
STATE DEPARTMENT OF EDUCATION
DIVISION OF VOCATIONAL EDUCATION

MIS 07D007

ACCIDENT REPORTING FORM FOR
VOCATIONAL EDUCATION COURSE/PROGRAM/ACTIVITY

INSTRUCTIONS:

1. Complete information and submit form within five (5) working days after the occurrence of the accident.
2. Only accidents requiring treatment by a licensed medical doctor are to be reported to the Division of Vocational Education.
3. The original report should be sent to:
   Director, Facilities/Equipment and Safety Control
   Division of Vocational Education
   New Jersey State Department of Education
   225 West State Street
   Trenton, New Jersey 08625
4. The first copy should be sent to the appropriate County Superintendent of Schools Office.
5. The second copy should be sent to the student's sending district, if appropriate.
6. The last copy should be retained by the originating school district.

SCHOOL INFORMATION

School Name______________________________

School Address______________________________

District______________________________

Telephone Number (Area Code)______________________________

PERSON INJURED______________________________SEX____M ____F
LAST FIRST MIDDLE

GRADE LEVEL__________AGE___STUDENT__________INSTRUCTOR________OTHER______(Specify)________

INJURED PERSON SENT TO______________HOSPITAL_________________PHYSICIAN

DATE OF ACCIDENT______________________________ TIME OF ACCIDENT____A.M. _____P.M.
MONTH DAY YEAR

LOCATION OF ACCIDENT IF OTHER THAN SCHOOL ADDRESS ABOVE:

____

____

____

TYPE OF VOCATIONAL COURSE/PROGRAM/ACTIVITY

*___Agriculture/Agribusiness/Natural Resources
*___Business Education
*___Cooperative Education
*___Consumer and Homemaking Education
*___Distributive Education
___Employment Orientation
*___Health Occupations
*___Home Economics Related Occupations
*___Introduction to Vocations
*___Industrial Arts
*___Technical Education
___Technology for Children
*___Vocational-Industrial Education
*___Work Study
___WECEP
*___Vocational Student Organizations
**___Other(Specify)
**______________________________

*Provide specific title of
course, program or activity______________________________

[523-5 (11/77)]

MIS 07D007

PART OF BODY INJURED

___Abdomen
___Ankle
___Arm
___Back
___Buttocks
___Chest
___Collar-Bone
___Ear
___Elbow
___Eye
___Face
___Finger
___Foot
___Hand
___Knee
___Leg
___Mouth
___Neck
___Nose
___Ribs
___Scalp
___Stomach
___Throat
___Teeth
___Wrist
*___Other

*SPECIFY________________________

APPARENT NATURE OF INJURY

___Abrasion
___Amputation
___Asphyxiation
___Bite
___Bruise
___Bump
___Burn
___Concussion
___Cut-Laceration
___Dislocation
___Fracture
___Poisoning
___Puncture
___Scalding
___Scratches
___Shock(electric)
___Splinter
___Sprain
___Sting
*___Other

*SPECIFY________________________

CAUSE OF INJURY

___Struck Against
___Struck By
___Fall from Elevation
___Fall from Same Level
___Caught In, Under, Between
___Rubbed or Abraded
___Overexertion
___Other(Specify)________________________
___Contact with Electric Current
___Contact with Caustic, Toxic, Noxious Substance
___Contact with Temperature Extremes

DEGREE OF INJURY

___Non-Disabling
___Temporary Disability
___Permanent Disability
___Death

NARRATIVE (Briefly describe how accident occurred indicating conditions, actions, tools and equipment involved.)

____
____
____
____
____

COOPERATIVE EDUCATION ACCIDENTS ONLY

Was Student Covered By	YES	NO
Working Papers	___	___
Training Agreement	___	___
Workman's Compensation	___	___

Student's Job Title:________________________

____

ACCIDENT REPORT COMPLETED BY:

Name________________________
Title________________________
Telephone Number________________________
Date________________________

*Signature of Principal or Superintendent

*________________________

Date________________________

Page 2 of 2

APPENDIX F

Eye-Witness Report Form

Name of pupil injured____________________________ Date_________

Course and room number__________________________ Time_________

1. What was the nature of the activity engaged in at the time of the accident?
2. What piece of equipment, tool, or material was involved in the accident?
3. Had safety instructions been given the class concerning this?
4. Was another person involved in the accident? If so, in what manner?
5. Where were you in relation to the injured person at the time of the accident? Were you able to see clearly just what happened?
6. Was the injured pupil violating any safety instructions at the time of his injury?
7. In your own words, what person, tool, or circumstance was responsible for this accident?
8. To the best of your knowledge, what was the extent of the injury?
9. What care was given the injured pupil following the accident?
10. Was any personal protective equipment involved in the injury?

____

Signature of person filling out report

APPENDIX G

Eye-Safety Legislation

State	*Effective or Approval Date*	*Specifies ANSI Code Z-2, 1-1959 or Z87.1-1968-1979*	*Colleges & Universities*	*Private Schools*	*Visitors & Observers*	*Enforcement Provisions*	*Sanitation Requirement*	*Required Guidelines*	*No Provision for Acquisition*	*Board May Provide*	*Board Shall Provide*
Alabama	April 1965	X			X						X
Alaska											
Arizona	July 1968	X	X	X	X			X			X
Arkansas	Sept. 1965	X	X							X	
California	July 1965	X		X	X	X				X	
Colorado	Sept. 1969	X	X	X	X	X		X			X
Connecticut	July 1967			X				X	X		
Delaware	July 1966	X	X	X	X			X	X		
District of Columbia	May 1970	X		X		X					X
Florida	June 1965	X	X		X			X		X	
Georgia	Feb. 1974		X		X			X			X
Hawaii											

State	*Effective or Approval Date*	*Specifies ANSI Code Z-2,1-1959 or Z87.1-1968-1979*	*Colleges & Universities*	*Private Schools*	*Visitors & Observers*	*Enforcement Provisions*	*Sanitation Requirement*	*Required Guidelines*	*No Provision for Acquisition*	*Board May Provide*	*Board Shall Provide*
Idaho											
Illinois	Aug. 1965	X	X		X			X		X	
Indiana	July 1967	X			X					X	
Iowa	May 1965*	X	X	X	X	X				X	
Kansas	April 1967	X	X		X					X	
Kentucky											
Louisiana	July 1966										X
Maine	State-wide School Eye Safety by Department of Education directive										
Maryland	June 1965	X			X					X	
Massachusetts	Feb. 1964				X				X		
Michigan	Sept. 1972	X			X		X	X			X
Minnesota	Jan. 1968	X	X		X	X				X	
Mississippi	March 1974	X	X		X					X	
Missouri	Sept. 1974	X	X	X	X					X	
Montana											
Nebraska											
Nevada											
New Hampshire											
New Jersey	July 1965	X			X	X		X	X		
New Mexico	State-wide School Eye Safety by Department of Education directive										

*Amended 1970.

State	*Effective or Approval Date*	*Specifies ANSI Code Z-2, 1-1959 or Z87.1-1968-1979*	*Colleges & Universities*	*Private Schools*	*Visitors & Observers*	*Enforcement Provisions*	*Sanitation Requirement*	*Required Guidelines*	*No Provision for Acquisition*	*Board May Provide*	*Board Shall Provide*
New York	Sept. 1966			X	X			X	X		
North Carolina	July 1969	X		X	X						X
North Dakota											
Ohio	Aug. 1963*	X	X	X	X					X	
Oklahoma	Feb. 1969	X	X	X	X			X		X	
Oregon											
Pennsylvania	July 1965	X	X	X	X	X		X			X
Rhode Island	Feb. 1966		X	X	X			X			X
South Carolina	June 1965	X			X						X
South Dakota	1969	X		X	X						X
Tennessee	July 1967	X	X						X		
Texas	July 1965									X	
Utah	Jan. 1965	X			X					X	
Vermont											
Virginia	Mar. 1966	X	X	X	X					X	
Washington	April 1969	X	X	X	X			X			X
West Virginia											
Wisconsin	July 1973	X	X	X	X			X		X	
Wyoming	Feb. 1967	X			X						X

*Amended 1972.

APPENDIX H

Model School Eye-Safety Law

THE following text is offered by the National Society for the Prevention of Blindness, Inc.* as a guide in planning and preparing legislation to require state-wide eye safety for all students and teachers using or visiting school and college laboratory and shop facilities. Comparable protection for the eyesight of visitors to such educational areas is also advocated.

An Act to enact legislation requiring all students and teachers to wear approved eye protective devices when participating in certain vocational, industrial arts, and chemical-physical laboratory courses of instruction.

Be it enacted by the legislature of the State of____________________:

SECTION 1. Every student and teacher in schools, colleges, universities, or other educational institutions, participating in or observing any of the following courses of instruction:

(A) Vocational, technical, industrial arts, chemical, or chemical-physical, involving exposure to:

1. Hot molten metals, or other molten materials;
2. Milling, sawing, turning, shaping, cutting, grinding, or stamping of any solid materials;
3. Heat treatment, tempering, or kiln firing of any metal or other materials;
4. Gas or electric arc welding, or other forms of welding processes;
5. Repair or servicing of any vehicle;
6. Caustic or explosive materials;

(B) Chemical, physical, or combined chemical-physical laboratories involving caustic or explosive materials, hot liquids or solids, injurious radiations, or other hazards not enumerated;

is required to wear appropriate industrial quality eye-protective devices at all times while participating in or observing such courses of instruction. Such

*National Society for the Prevention of Blindness, Inc., 79 Madison Ave., New York, N.Y. 10016.

devices may be furnished for all students and teachers, purchased and sold at cost to students and teachers, or made available for a moderate rental fee, and shall be furnished for all visitors to such shops and laboratories.

"Industrial quality eye protective devices," as used in this section, means devices meeting the standards of the *American National Standard Practice for Occupational and Educational Eye and Face Protection, Z87.1-1968,* and subsequent revisions thereof, approved by the American National Standards Institute, Inc.

The State Commissioner or Superintendent of Public Instruction, or other appropriate educational authority shall prepare and circulate to each public and private educational institution in this State instructions and recommendations for implementing the eye-safety provisions of this law.

APPENDIX I

Selected Bibliography

Books

Alexander, Kern; Ray Corns; and Walter McCann. *Public School Law.* St. Paul: West Publishing Company, 1969.

Berkowitz, Monroe. *Workmen's Compensation.* New Brunswick, N.J.: Rutgers University Press, 1960.

Binford, Charles M.; Cecil S. Flemming; and Z. A. Prust. *Loss Control in the OHSA Era.* New York: McGraw-Hill, 1975.

Delon, Floyd G. *School Officials and the Courts: Update 1979.* Arlington, Va.: Educational Research Service Inc., 1979.

Drury, Robert L., and Kenneth C. Ray. *Principles of School Law.* New York: Appleton-Century-Crofts, 1965.

Education Commmission of the States. *1973 State Education, Legislation, and Activity—Schools, Students and Services.* Denver, 1974.

Education Commission of the States. *1974 State Education, Legislation, and Activity—General Governance and Administration.* Denver, 1975.

Edwards, Newton. *The Courts and the Public Schools.* University of Chicago Press, 1955.

Florio, A.E., and G. T. Stafford. *Safety Education.* New York: McGraw-Hill, 1956.

Flowers, Anne, and Edward C. Bolmeier. *Law and Pupil Control.* Cincinnati, Ohio: The W. H. Anderson Company, 1964.

Garber, Lee O. *Handbook of School Law.* New London, Conn.: Arthur C. Croft Publications, 1954

_____. *Yearbook of School Law.* Philadelphia: School of Education, University of Pennsylvania, 1956

_____. *Yearbook of School Law.* Danville, Ill.: Interstate Printers and Publishers, Inc., 1957, 1958, 1961, and 1962.

_____, ed. *Law and the School Business Manager.* Danville, Ill.: Interstate Printers and Publishers, Inc., 1957.

_____; Robert L. Drury; and Roger M. Shaw. *The Law and the Ohio Teacher.* Danville, Ill.: Interstate Printers and Publishers, Inc., 1956.

Gatti, Daniel J., and Richard D. Gatti. *The Teacher and the Law*. West Nyack, N.Y.: Parker Publishing Co., 1972.

Gauerke, Warren E. *Legal and Ethical Responsibilities of School Personnel*. Englewood Cliffs, N.J.: Prentice-Hall, Inc., 1959.

Godbey, Frank W., ed. *Occupational Safety and Health in Vocational Education*. Cincinnati: U.S. Department of Health, Education, and Welfare—National Institute for Occupational Safety and Health, Division of Technical Services, 1979.

Greene, Mark R. *Risk and Insurance*. 4th ed. Cincinnati: South-Western Publishing Company, 1977.

Hamilton, Robert R. *Legal Rights and Liabilities of Teachers*. Laramie, Wyo.: Mountain States Lithographing Company, 1956.

——, and Paul R. Mort. *The Law and Public Education*. Brooklyn, N.Y.: The Foundation Press, Inc., 1959.

Hazard, William R. *Education and the Law*. New York: The Free Press, 1971.

Henson, Ray D., ed. *Landmarks of Law*. New York: Harper and Brothers, 1960.

Hollander, Patricia A. *Legal Handbook for Educators*. Boulder: Westview Press, 1978.

Kearney, Nolan C. *A Teacher's Professional Guide*. Englewood Cliffs, N.J.: Prentice-Hall, Inc., 1958.

Keesecker, Ward W. *Know Your School Law*. Washington, D.C.: Department of Health, Education, and Welfare, 1958.

Lowrance, William W. *Of Acceptable Risk*. Los Altos, Cal.: William Kaufman, Inc., 1976.

National Education Association. *The Teacher and the Law*. Washington, D.C.: NEA Research Division, 1959.

Nolte, M. Chester. *School Law in Action: 101 Key Decisions with Guidelines for School Administrators*. West Nyack, N.Y.: Parker Publishing Company, Inc., 1971.

Peterson, Le Roy; Richard A. Rossmiller; and Marlin M. Volz. *The Law and Public School Operation*. 2d ed. New York: Harper & Row Publishers, Inc., 1978.

Poe, Arthur C."School Liability for Injuries to Pupils." Dissertation, Columbia University, 1941.

Powell, Theodore. *The School Bus Law*. Middletown, Conn.: Wesleyan University Press, 1960.

Remmlein, Madaline K. *School Law*. New York: McGraw-Hill, 1950.

——. *School Law*. 2d ed. Danville, Ill.: Interstate Printers and Publishers, Inc., 1962.

——. *The Law of Local Public School Administration*. New York: McGraw-Hill, 1953.

Roady, Thomas G., Jr., and William R. Anderson, eds. *Professional Negligence*. Nashville, Tenn.: Vanderbilt University Press, 1960.

Rosenfield, Harry N. *Liability for School Accidents*. New York: Harper and Brothers, 1940.

Schaerer, Robert W. *The Liability Status of Indiana Public Schools.* Bloomington: Indiana School Boards Association, 1959.

Seaton, Don Cash; Herbert J. Stack; and Bernard I. Loft. *Administration and Supervision of Safety Education.* New York: The MacMillan Company, 1969.

Seitz, Reynolds C., ed. *Law and the School Principal.* Cincinnati, Ohio: W. H. Anderson Company, 1961.

Silvius, G. Harold, and Estell H. Curry. *Teaching Successfully the Industrial Arts and Vocational Subjects.* Bloomington, Ind.: McKnight and McKnight Publishing Company, 1953.

Stack, Herbert J., and Elmer B. Siebrecht. *Education for Safe Living.* New York: Prentice-Hall, Inc., 1942.

Strasser, Marland K.; James E. Aaron; Ralph C. Bohn; and John R. Eales. *Fundamentals of Safety Education.* New York: The MacMillan Company, 1964.

Williams, William A., ed. *Accident Prevention Manual for Shop Teachers.* Chicago: American Technical Society, 1963.

Williams, J.E., and C.L. Brownell. *Administration of Health and Physical Education.* Philadelphia: W. B. Saunders Company, 1946.

Pamphlets

Accident Prevention Can Be Learned. New York: Metropolitan Life Insurance Company, 1962.

American Association of School Administrators. *Managing the School District Insurance Program.* Washington: National Education Association, 1953.

_____. *School District Liability.* Washington: National Education Association, 1953.

Connecticut Laws Relating to Education. Hartford: Connecticut State Board of Education, 1950.

Hamilton, Robert R. *The Bi-Weekly School Law Letter.* Laramie, Wyo.: College of Law, University of Wyoming. Vol. 1, March 1951; Vol. 1, No. 5, April 1951; Vol. 3, No. 5, April 1953; Vol. 4, No. 14, September 1954.

Industrial Safety Education in Schools. New York: Metropolitan Life Insurance Company, March 1949.

Laws Relating to the Minnesota Public School System. St. Paul: Minnesota State Department of Education, 1953.

Kigin, Denis J. *Tort Liability Affecting Shop Teachers with Provisions for Avoiding Accidents and Litigation.* Columbia, Mo.: The University of Missouri Bulletin, January 1960.

Leibee, Howard C. *Developments in Legal Liability for Accidents and Accident Insurance.* Daytona Beach, Fla.: Proceedings of the College Physical Education Association, 1956.

National Education Association. *The Legal Status of the Public-School Pupil.* Washington: Research Bulletin, February 1948.

_____. *The Legal Status of the Public-School Teacher.* Washington: Research Bulletin, April 1947.

———. *Teacher Liability for Pupil Injuries*. Washington: Research Bulletin, April 1940.

———. *The Teacher's Day in Court*. Washington: Research Division, Review of 1963, 1964, 1965, 1966, 1967, 1968, 1969, 1970 and 1971.

———. *Who is Liable for Pupil Injuries?* Washington: Research Division, October 1950.

Remmlein, Madaline K. *Law and Contemporary Problems*. Durham, N.C.: Duke University School of Law, Winter 1955.

Safety Education in the School Shop. Chicago: National Safety Council, 1948.

School Laws of Pennsylvania. Harrisburg, Pa.: Department of Public Instruction, Commonwealth of Pennsylvania, 1953.

Swalls, Fred. *Legal Aspects of Student Teaching*. Danville, Ill.: Interstate Printers and Publishers, 1966.

Woodward, Robert L. *Safety Instruction in Industrial Arts Education*. Sacramento: California State Department of Education, 1955.

Periodicals

Anderson, Stuart A. "Danger Zones in Shop Safety." *Industrial Arts and Vocational Education,* October 1955.

Archer, Glynn R., and Joseph M. Leps. "School Employees are Legally Vulnerable." *School Management,* March 1961.

Bacher, Robert E. "Liability in a Private Boarding School." *The Catholic Educational Review,* February 1961.

Biggam, William R. "Eye Safety Legislation." *School Shop*, April 1972.

Bolmeier, E.C. "Tort Liability of School Personnel." *American School Board Journal*, March 1958.

Bowen, Frank, Jr. "Negligence—Foreseeability as Limitation on Liability." *Michigan Law Review*, January 1952.

Caldwell, David R. "RHAM-Ahead to Safety." *School Shop*, April 1972.

Chambers, M.M. "Current Decisions on School Law." *Nation's Schools*, July 1948.

Cohler, Milton J. "The Law, The Teacher and The Child." *American School Board Journal*, October 1951; November 1951; December 1951; February 1952; March 1952.

Coleman, Gerald M. "Who Is Responsible for This Accident?" *Safety Education*, February 1950.

Corwin, John K. "PMI for Electrical Safety." *School Shop*, April 1972.

Doscher, Nathan, and Nelson Walke."The Status of Liability for School Physical Education Accidents and Its Relationship to the Health Program." *Research Quarterly*, October 1952.

Entorf, John F. "Shop Safety Devices." *School Shop*, April 1972.

Faulkner, L.A. "The High Cost of Eye Injuries." *American Machinist*, March 5, 1962.

Fishman, Irving S. "Torts—Liability of Insured School District." *University of Illinois Law Review*, Spring 1953.

Foster, Charles W. "What's Ahead in School Safety." *School Shop*, April 1972.

Gallop, A.L. "MEA Insurance Services." *Minnesota Journal of Education*, October 1956.

Garber, Lee O. "Save Harmless Statutes." *Nation's Schools*, June 1957.

_____ . "Illinois Court Overthrows Immunity Doctrine." *Nation's Schools*, August 1959. Same condensed: *The Education Digest*, November 1959.

_____ . "How the Courts Are Changing the Education Scene." *Nation's Schools*, January 1962. Same condensed: *The Education Digest*, April 1962.

Gausman, Chester A. "Legal Aspects of Shop Accidents." *Industrial Arts and Vocational Education*, September 1955.

Giles, John W. "Liability of Coaches and Athletic Instructors."*Athletic Journal*, February 1962.

Hamburg, Merrill C. "The AIAA Gives Leadership to Teacher Liability Program." *Industrial Arts Teacher*, October 1952.

Hamilton, Robert R. "School Liability." *Safety Education,* December 1952.

_____ . "Teachers and Tort Liability." *Illinois Education*, September 1956.

Hogan, Howard K. "Using School Shops to Develop Safety Consciousness in Tomorrow's Workers." *School Life*, May 1959.

Hubbard, Frank W. "Teacher Liability and Insurance Protection." *Industrial Arts Teacher*, June 1953.

Hughes, Wayne P. " The School Shop Accident Situation." *Industrial Arts Teacher*, June 1958.

Johnston, Wallace L. "The Law and School Shops." *School Shop*, February 1975.

Kigin, Denis J. "Cases of the Negligent Teacher." *Mississippi Educational Advance*, April 1965.

_____ . "Compare School Program to Established Criteria." *The American School Board Journal*, July 1967.

_____ . "Damage Claims and School-Shop Accidents." *School Shop*, January 1963.

_____ . "Eye Safety and Student Attitudes." *Journal of Industrial Teacher Education*, Spring 1965.

_____ . "Eye Safety and Teacher Liability." *School Shop*, September 1973.

_____ . "Liability: Are You Responsible?" *School Shop*, April 1972.

_____ . "The Prevention of Liability—A Corollary of Safety." *Industrial Arts and Vocational Education*, February 1962.

_____ . "School Eye Injuries and Teacher Liability." *The Sight Saving Review*, Fall 1967.

_____ . "Sight Preservation—An Educational Mandate." *Safety*, May-June 1966.

_____ . "Ten Cases of the Negligent Teacher." *Safety Education*, December 1964.

_____ . "The Second Effort." *Safety Newsletter*, January-February 1967.

_____ . "What You Should Know About Shop Teacher Liability." *Industrial Arts and Vocational Education*, September 1960.

_____ . "Who Pays for School Shop Accidents?" *Safety Education*, December 1961. Same condensed: *The Education Digest*, February 1962.

_____ . "Would You Be Liable If . . ." *Safety Education*, February 1964.

———, with Lynn D. Wilson. "Accident Prevention and the Embryo Engineer." *Industrial Management*, Part I, May 1972 and Part II, June 1972.

Koble, Ronald L. "Governmental Immunity Laws: New Implications for Shop Teachers." *School Shop*, March 1980.

Krejcie, Robert V. "Developing Safety Attitudes." *School Shop*, April 1972.

Leipold, L.E. "Four Steps to Understanding School Law." *American School Board Journal*, June 1958.

———. "The Law Enters the Classroom." *American School Board Journal*, April 1949.

"Liability Insurance." *Michigan Education Journal*, March 1954.

Moran, Kenneth, and Christopher V. Sylvester. "Negligence." *North Dakota Law Review*, April 1954.

Nichols, George V., Jr. "The Psychology of Safety." *School Shop*, April 1972.

Olsen, Fred A. "Student Injuries and Teacher Liability." *School Shop*, Part I, October 1960 and Part II, November 1960.

Pfister, Richard G. "Shop Safety and the Job Safety Laws." *School Shop*, April 1972.

Piilo, Herbert E. "Are Shop Teachers Liable?" *Safety Education*, May 1951.

"Plaintiffs and Defendants." *Research Bulletin of the National Education Association*, April 1958.

Prasinos, Nicholas. "Designing for Safety." *Mechanical Engineering*, May 1958.

Proehl, Paul O. "Tort Liability of Teachers." *Vanderbilt Law Review*, June 1959.

Radtke, R.A. "Liability Suit Won by Teacher." *Industrial Arts and Vocational Education*, April 1954.

Rathbun, Jesse E. "Moral and Legal Aspects of Safety Education." *Industrial Arts and Vocational Education*, November 1946.

Reutter, E. Edmund, Jr. "Tort Liability of the School District." *American School Board Journal*, March 1958.

Rice, S.W. "Suit for the Teacher." *Journal of Health, Physical Education, and Recreation*, November 1961.

Roach, S.F. "School District Tort Immunity, Overruled." *American School Board Journal*, October 1959.

Rosenfield, Harry H. "Legal Liability and the Cost of Accidents." *Safety Education*, April 1957.

———. "Liability for School Accidents." *Nation's Schools*, June 1947 and June 1948.

Satterfield, Ted J. "The Teacher Pays." *Phi Delta Kappan*, September 1950.

Seitz, Reynolds C. "When Are You Responsible for Pupils?" *The Catholic School Journal*, November 1959.

Shaw, Roger M. "In Loco Parentis." *The School Executive*, May 1955.

Smith, William W. "From Immunity Toward Liability of Parochial Schools." *The Catholic Educational Review*, October 1961.

———. "Trend Toward Tort Liability." *Catholic School Journal*, November 1961.

Stacy, James, ed. "OSHA Seeks Aid in Job Safety." *Journal of American Insurance*, Fall 1972.

Tischendorf, E.W. "Accident Liability of Shop Teachers." *Safety Education*,

February 1951.
_____. "Shop Teacher Liability." *School Shop*, February 1953.
_____. "You May Be Liable." *School Shop*, April 1952.
Tooze, Walter J. "Contributory Versus Comparative Negligence—A Judge Expresses His Views." *NACCA Law Journal*, November 1953.
Walgren, John. "Are Shop Teachers Liable for Accidents?" *School Shop*, December 1956.
Walsh, J. Hartt, and Lowell M. Johnson. "Courts Favor Student Activities." *Nation's Schools*, December 1947.
Ware, Martha L. "Is the Teacher Liable?" *National Education Association Journal*, December 1958.
Williams, William A. "Teaching Practices for Accident Prevention." *School Shop*, April 1972.
_____. "Shop Safety Rules and Regulations." *School Shop*, April 1972.

Unpublished Materials

Culbertson, Arley B. "Liability with Reference to Teachers in Industrial Education for Damages Resulting from Injuries to Pupils Under Their Supervision." Master's thesis, Kansas State Teachers College, Pittsburg, Kansas, 1954.
D'Ovidio, Anthony A. "Shop Accident Liability Protection for Kansas Industrial Education Teachers." Master's thesis, Kansas State Teachers College, Emporia, Kansas, 1954
Foster, Milton M. "Tort Liability Affecting the Industrial Arts Teacher." Master's thesis, Oregon State College, Corvallis, Oregon, 1952.
Henderson, Bob Ray. "A Study of the Aspects of Shop Teacher Liability." Master's thesis, Oklahoma Agricultural and Mechanical College, Stillwater, Oklahoma, 1956.
Kigin, Denis J. "Tort Liability Affecting Shop Teachers with Provisions for Avoiding Accidents and Litigation." Doctoral dissertation, University of Missouri, Columbia, 1959.
Nelson, Clyde August. "A Checklist of Minimum Essentials of Safety Education Needed in Preparation of Prospective Industrial Education Teachers." Master's thesis, Chicago Teachers College, Chicago, 1958.
Pinckey, Charles W. "Liabilities of Shop Teachers and School Districts for Pupil Injuries in School Shops Resulting in Court Cases in the United States." Doctoral dissertation, Pennsylvania State College, University Park, 1953.

Index